WHY Cannot?

Scriptural View of Christians Dating and Marrying Non-Christians

DR CHOA CHANG LOONG

*Special thanks
to my wife,
Tan Ai Cheng
for her unwavering support,
without which this book
would not have been possible.*

CONTENTS

Why Is This Such A Huge Problem?

The apostle Paul warns the church in Corinth to guard against unequally yoked relationships (2 Cor. 6:14). This term is often associated with spiritually unhealthy partnerships between Christians and non-Christians, particularly in the marriage context. In his book *The Unequal Yoke*, David Wong offers a definition:

> The unequal yoke then, has to be clearly understood. A yoke refers to a partnership where two or more parties join hands and walk together. When they are fundamentally different, they will invariably walk in different directions. We have applied this to business as well as ecclesiastical partnerships. Fateful as such unequal yokes may be, they cannot compare in seriousness with the third kind of partnership – marriage. In the former two partnerships, liaisons made can be terminated. In marriage, it is for life, till death ends the partnership. Marriage is a partnership that lasts a lifetime. Once committed, husband and wife will walk together, for better or for worse, for as long as they live. With an

unequal yoke, the road ahead for them presents thorny issues and difficult challenges.[1]

This warning still holds tremendous relevance to the churches of today, as it did during Paul's time.

In an interview with *Christianity Today*, Russell Moore laments about the less-than-ideal situation of believers marrying unbelievers in an unequally yoked union. He concludes with these words: "A marriage of a follower of Christ to an unbeliever impedes the intimacy of a union that, from the beginning, was intended to be about a common mission under the rule of a common King (Gen. 1:27-28)."[2] An unequally yoked romance is not what God intended and inhibits the gospel mission of the church. In their book *Boundaries in Dating*, Henry Cloud and John Townsend also make a similar observation:

> Christians need to be very involved in the real world, as agents of God's love. This is what being salt and light are about (Matthew 5:13-16). At the same time, the deepest and most significant part of you needs to find a home in the heart of the most important human relationship in your life (2 Corinthians 6:14). Because of this, we believe that Christians should not be in serious dating relationships with non-Christians.[3]

This uncomfortable topic of Christians being romantically involved with non-Christians is a frequent lament echoed by

---

[1] David W. F. Wong, *The Unequal Yoke: When Two May Not Walk Together* (Singapore: Genesis Books, 2013), 6.

[2] Mark Regnerus, Naomi Schaefer Riley, and Russell D. Moore. "Biblical Bonding: Is Interfaith Marriage Always Wrong, Given That the Bible Teaches Us Not to Be 'Unequally Yoked'?" *Christianity Today* 57, no. 5 (June 2013): 63.

[3] Henry Cloud and John Townsend, *Boundaries in Dating: How Healthy Choices Grow Healthy Relationships* (Grand Rapids: Zondervan, 2000), 66.

churches of all sizes and denominational affiliations. Yet there are still many churches out there that have hardly offered any teaching on unequally yoked relationships to their congregation, particularly their youth and young adults, leaving them to be unsure of what sort of stand to take with regard to the possibility of getting romantically attached to a non-Christian. These youth and young adults are at an age where they are starting to think about dating and romance seriously. Yet, at such a crucial juncture of their life, they are not armed with what the Bible teaches on this subject; they lack pastoral guidance in forming biblically grounded convictions on these matters of the heart. Especially in churches where adult church members with non-Christian spouses are actively serving, even in leadership and teaching positions, resulting in their youth and young adults lacking exemplary role models in their own churches. This makes it doubly important for the youth and young adults' views on unequally yoked relationships to be shaped by what the Bible says about it rather than what they see in their church environment. Ultimately, the church needs to be rooted in what the Bible says about unequally yoked romantic relationships–whether God thinks it is acceptable or it is a sin. We also need to help them learn how to be loving and sympathetic toward those who are already in such relationships.

In churches where there is a lack of teaching on this subject of unequally yoked relationships and where the presence of unequally yoked relationships is commonplace, dating and marrying a non-Christian remain as very real options for church members especially if the church chooses to stay silent on the subject. Therefore, it is important to break the silence and help people see what God thinks about unequally yoked relationships. This book serves to allow the teaching of the Scriptures to convince people; that they may know through the Scriptures if unequally yoked relationships are a sin or not and how a wrong decision in this matter can impact their lives spiritually and practically. Undergirding this endeavor are three theological concepts. The first of these concepts underscores the teaching of Scriptures with regard to unequally yoked relationships–what the Word of God instructs with regard to God's people marrying outside of the covenant community from the Old Testament to the New Testament. The second considers how marriage between two Christians is God's ideal for spiritually healthy marriages. The final one looks at how obedience to God's Word on marriage relationships is crucial to joy and fulfilment for the believer.

PART 1

Why Would God Disapprove of Interfaith Marriages?

1

A GOLDEN CHAIN

In describing marriage between a Christian and a non-Christian, the term "interfaith marriage" is preferable as opposed to "mixed marriage." This is because "mixed marriage" in modern terms can also refer to interracial marriages. While Christians of any race should have the freedom to date and marry interracially as long as both are believers, they "do not have the freedom to enter such a relationship with unbelievers."[4] However, interfaith marriage can also be a reference to marriages from other religions, like a Buddhist marrying a Hindu. Therefore, to avoid confusion, in the course of this book, whenever "interfaith marriage" is used, it shall be in reference to God's covenant community marrying outside of the covenant community.

The most fundamental passage dealing with God's prohibition of interfaith marriage lies in Exod. 34:11-17, where it forms part of Moses's law. This prohibition is especially highlighted in verse 16: "and you take of their daughters for your sons, and their daughters whore after their gods and make your

---

[4] George A. Yancey, "Unequally Yoked by Race or by Faith?" *Criswell Theological Review* 6, no. 2 (Spr 2009): 75.

sons whore after their gods." The reason for the prohibition is explicitly mentioned here. Interfaith marriage will cause God's covenant people to be influenced and drawn away from worshiping the true God and lean toward false gods. Interfaith marriage is thus seen here as a breeding ground for idolatry. In his observation of the culture in those days surrounding this text in verse 16, Douglas Stuart says:

> Over time young men and young women would meet each other and ask their parents to arrange their marriages (as in the prominent example of Samson in Judg 14:1–10), so it would be almost inevitable that as international marriages then took place, those marriages would bring idolatry into Israel. It happened that way with Solomon (1 Kgs 11:3–4) because marriages in Bible times, as today, were rarely blocked and often not even much discouraged for reasons of religious incompatibility. But Yahweh insisted otherwise here, knowing the inclinations of his people and the power of romantic attraction to overcome inadequate religious conviction.[5]

Deuteronomy 7:3-4 makes the interfaith marriage prohibition even clearer: "Do not intermarry with them. Do not give your daughters to their sons or take their daughters for your sons, for they will turn your children away from following me to serve other gods, and the Lord's anger will burn against you and will quickly destroy you" (Deut. 7:3-4 [NIV]). In this passage, a golden chain of events can be discerned. **The certainty of ungodly influence upon God's covenant community through interfaith marriage will lead to idolatry, which in turn leads to the arousal of God's anger,**

---

[5] Douglas K. Stuart, *Exodus, vol. 2*, The New American Commentary, ed. E. Ray Clendenen (Nashville: Holman Reference, 2006), VII, 1, 8, Olive Tree Bible Software.

leading ultimately to the destruction of God's people. In this instance, interfaith marriage is explicitly prohibited and along with the prohibition is the reason behind the prohibition. By forbidding interfaith marriages, God seeks to guard against any form of disruption of covenant faithfulness to himself by eradicating the temptation to follow the religious practices of foreign nations brought about by the intimate bonds of marriage.[6]

---

[6] Peter C. Craigie, *The Book of Deuteronomy,* New International Commentary on the Old Testament, ed. Robert L. Hubbard (Grand Rapids: Eerdmans Publishing, 1976), III, B, 6, Olive Tree Bible Software.

2

OLD TESTAMENT EXAMPLES

Numbers 25:1-15 renders for us a chilling account of how God dealt ever so severely with his people when they fell into the idolatrous practice of Baal worship. However, the chapter begins with a clear explanation of what led to such idolatry: "the people began to whore with the daughters of Moab" (v. 1). Sexual relations with foreign women inevitably led to idolatry, which led to the Lord's anger being kindled against Israel (v. 3). This sin of sexual relations with foreign women came to an apex when an Israelite man, Zimri, brought a Midianite woman, Cozbi, into the camp "in the sight of Moses and in the sight of the whole congregation of the people of Israel" (v. 6), in which case, they were publicly lamenting their act being called out as sin and also God's punishment of it (which is revealed as a plague in v. 8).[7] The death penalty, in the form of a plague (which eventually killed twenty-

---

[7] Timothy R. Ashley, *The Book of Numbers*, New International Commentary on the Old Testament, ed. Robert L. Hubbard (Grand Rapids: Eerdmans Publishing, 1993), V, B, 1. Olive Tree Bible Software.

four thousand) was invoked as a fitting punishment for all involved in the sin, but the fierce anger of the Lord was only averted when Phinehas, the son of Eleazar the high priest, in his zeal for the Lord, speared Zimri, together with Cozbi (v. 8). In the midst of God's judgment on Israel, Zimri had refused to repent of his involvement with foreign women and even upped the ante. The graphic violence that was recorded as a result of Zimri's rebellion against God's clear commands is thus a grim reminder of how God abhors idolatry and the path that leads to it, which in this case, is sexual relations with foreign women.

In 1 Kings 11:1-9, we see another consistent example of how God's people who get involved with women outside of the covenant community always end up in idolatry. This is another momentous account of how the many foreign women in King Solomon's life turned his heart away from God. In verse 2, God had already spoken, "'You shall not enter into marriage with them, neither shall they with you, for surely they will turn away your heart after their gods.'" The Word from the Lord is "surely," from the Hebrew "*aken,*" denoting certainty. True enough, Solomon "clung to these in love" (v. 3). As Scripture has already foretold, interfaith marriage leads to divided loyalties, preventing the king from having a wholehearted relationship with God.[8] The Bible goes on to record the Lord's emotions toward Solomon's actions: that of anger (v. 9). Such disobedience angers the Lord.

Another poignant example of the interfaith marriage of a king is King Ahab's union with Jezebel. 1 Kings 16:31 says, "And as if it had been a light thing for him to walk in the sins of Jeroboam the

---

[8] Donald J. Wiseman, *1 and 2 Kings,* Tyndale Old Testament Commentaries, ed. David G. Firth (Downers Grove: IVP Academic, 2008), 2, C, iv, a, Olive Tree Bible Software.

son of Nebat, he took for his wife Jezebel the daughter of Ethbaal king of the Sidonians, and went and served Baal and worshiped him." Jeroboam is the first king that led the newly divided kingdom of Israel into idolatry with two golden calves, one in Bethel and one in Dan (1 Kings 12:25-33). Therefore, the Scriptures attest that King Ahab, over and above committing idolatry like his grandfather (Jeroboam), went ahead and married a foreign wife, Jezebel. And again, the Scriptures consistently portray the evil influence this foreign wife had on King Ahab, which led him toward Baal worship. In verse 33, the Scriptures declare that "Ahab did more to provoke the Lord, the God of Israel, to anger than all the kings of Israel who were before him." **As can be seen in both King Solomon and King Ahab's testimony, interfaith marriage and idolatry are intricately interrelated, and they consistently result in God's anger.**

Turning to the books of Ezra and Nehemiah, again, we consistently see how interfaith marriage is considered an act whereby God's people "break faith" with their God. Such acts of unfaithfulness are tantamount to law-breaking and are dealt with "according to the Law."

> And Shecaniah the son of Jehiel, of the sons of Elam, addressed Ezra: "We have broken faith with our God and have married foreign women from the peoples of the land, but even now there is hope for Israel in spite of this. Therefore let us make a covenant with our God to put away all these wives and their children, according to the counsel of my lord and of those who tremble at the commandment of our God, and let it be done according to the Law (Ezra 10:2-3).

In Neh. 13:23-27, once again, we see that under the godly leadership of Nehemiah, interfaith marriage is duly condemned.

> In those days also I saw the Jews who had married women of Ashdod, Ammon, and Moab. And half of their children spoke the language of Ashdod, and they could not speak the language of Judah, but only the language of each people. And I confronted them and cursed them and beat some of them and pulled out their hair. And I made them take an oath in the name of God, saying, "You shall not give your daughters to their sons, or take their daughters for your sons or for yourselves. Did not Solomon king of Israel sin on account of such women? Among the many nations there was no king like him, and he was beloved by his God, and God made him king over all Israel. Nevertheless, foreign women made even him to sin. Shall we then listen to you and do all this great evil and act treacherously against our God by marrying foreign women?" (Neh. 13:23-27).

Nehemiah found his people's covenant-breaking act of marrying foreign women so detestable that he saw fit to confront those guilty of interfaith marriage; to even take such drastic actions as beating some of them up and "pulling out their hair."[9] Nehemiah's final resolution is to make them take an oath to never marry off their sons and daughters to foreigners (Neh. 13:25).

These various passages from the Old Testament particularly stand out as we confront this topic of interfaith marriages. The Israelites knew God's law against interfaith marriage and yet they knowingly went against God's law and intermarried outside of God's covenant community. Such disobedience provokes God to

---

[9] F. Charles Fensham, *The Books of Ezra and Nehemiah*, New International Commentary on the Old Testament, ed. Robert L. Hubbard (Grand Rapids: Eerdmans Publishing, 1983), VII, D, Olive Tree Bible Software.

anger and elicits drastic actions from godly leadership, as can be seen under the leadership of Ezra and Nehemiah.

Before we depart from the shores of the Old Testament, something must be said of the many intermarriages (or sexual involvement) of notable biblical figures who entered such relationships by choice. Abraham impregnated Sarah's Egyptian maidservant, Hagar (Gen. 16:4); Judah married a Canaanite woman (Gen. 38:2); Joseph married the daughter of an Egyptian priest, Asenath (Gen. 41:45); Moses married the daughter of a Midianite priest, Zipporah (Exod. 2:21); Moses later married a Cushite woman (Num. 12:1); Boaz married a Moabite woman, Ruth (Ruth 4:13). With regard to Esther's intermarriage to Ahasuerus the Persian king, this would not form part of the list, as she likely did not enter into the marriage by choice but was rather drafted into the king's harem (Esther 1:8).

In all of these intermarriages (or sexual relations) that were entered in by choice, Fanie Snyman notes that none of them endured any form of negative comments from the narrator even though intermarriage was forbidden in the legal parts of the Pentateuch. [10] A possible explanation for such a discrepancy between the law against intermarriage and the practice of intermarriages by these notable figureheads is that the Scripture assumed that all these foreign women who marry such prominent figures in Israelite history would naturally become worshippers of Yahweh, as is the case for Ruth.[11] **This would certainly eradicate Yahweh's concern of intermarriage being the catalyst for**

---

[10] Fanie Snyman, "Investigating the Issue of Mixed Marriages in Malachi, Ezra-Nehemiah and the Pentateuch," *Scriptura* 116, no. 2 (2017): 183.

[11] Snyman, "Investigating," 183.

idolatry and reinforce the fact that the prohibition is not against ethnicity per se but against idolatry.

3

WHAT ABOUT INTERFAITH MARRIAGES UNDER THE NEW COVENANT?

Having examined the Old Testament Scriptures, we now turn to the New Testament to see if the clear prohibition of interfaith marriages in the Old Testament does carry over to the New Testament era.

First Cor. 7:39 specifically addresses the context of marriage. "A woman is bound to her husband as long as he lives. But if her husband dies, she is free to marry anyone she wishes, but he must belong to the Lord" (1 Cor. 7:39 [NIV]). In this verse, Paul is giving instructions to widows, telling them that if they were to remarry, they must make sure that their new spouses "belong to the Lord"– that their new spouses must be Christians. Paul offers full freedom to widows to remarry "anyone she wishes," but with a proviso added. Anthony Thiselton notes that the meaning of this proviso has been much debated among scholars.

> The principle that if a spouse has died the remaining partner is free to re-marry is qualified by the phrase μόνον ἐν κυρίῳ. Against our inclination we have left the translation as open-ended as the Greek, in order not to pre-judge an interpretation, as far as possible. Most English translations retain only in the Lord, although NIV explicates he must belong to the Lord, and REB, within the Lord's fellowship. For the meaning is disputed. J.-J. von Allmen thinks it means, "without her [the widow who remarries] being excluded from the body of Christ." Most interpreters, however, but not all, see this as a proviso addressed to the widow specifying that the remarriage is legitimate only if it is to a Christian believer. This is the view of many. A small minority insist that "the expression cannot be so pressed. . . . She must remember that she is a member of Christ's body and not forget her Christian duties."[12]

Thiselton highlights the fact that most scholars do agree with NIV's explication and concludes his own analysis of μόνον ἐν κυρίῳ by opting for the marriage to a Christian believer as the preferred meaning based on the overall arguments presented by Paul in the reading of chapter seven in its entirety. This is how he puts it:

> But after all that Paul has said about lack of distraction such a meaning would be banal, and would contradict any notion that freedom to be devoted to the Lord as a single, celibate person could be balanced against the opportunity to serve the Lord with

---

[12] Anthony C. Thiselton, *The First Epistle to the Corinthians,* The New International Greek Testament Commentary, ed. Mark Goodacre and Todd D. Still (Grand Rapids: Eerdmans Publishing, 2013), IV, A, 7, Olive Tree Bible Software.

the mutual support of a Christian spouse. This view is well supported (Senft, Héring, Fee, et al.). The only mixed marriages which Paul countenances are existing ones; to marry an unbeliever would indeed be to invite a pull in two directions and a lack of unified vision. Bruce believes that marriage to a fellow-Christian is "probably implied." But the principle of "marriage" with a Christian (Senft) or "a Christian marriage" (Héring) is demanded not so much by the syntax of this verse as by the perspective of the whole chapter. The alternative is "unthinkable" (Fee).[13]

Thomas Schreiner also concurs, offering an instructive tone pertaining to this pivotal phrase μόνον ἐν κυρίῳ.

> Still, Paul adds a final qualification: she is to marry 'only in the Lord' (csb), which the NIV rightly translates as: he must belong to the Lord. The wife may marry anyone she prefers to marry, but the man must be a believer. She is not free to marry a man who is an unbeliever. Apparently, a woman who belongs to and loves Christ expresses her Christian faith by marrying a person of the opposite sex who also belongs to Jesus Christ.[14]

Schreiner provides an emphatic certainty to μόνον ἐν κυρίῳ by using firm language–"the man must be a believer" and "She is not free…." In contrast, Gordon Fee offers a softer approach to μόνον ἐν κυρίῳ by stating that it "is not so much a command that she may not marry outside the Lord as it is good sense."[15] Fee elaborates on his notion of "good sense" by explaining that a Christian widow "lives from such a radically different perspective and value system

---

[13] Thiselton, *Corinthians*, IV, A, 7.

[14] Thomas R. Schreiner, *1 Corinthians*, Tyndale New Testament Commentaries, ed. David G. Firth (Downers Grove: IVP Academic, 2018), 162.

[15] Gordon D. Fee, *The First Epistle to the Corinthians*, New International Commentary on the New Testament, eds. Ned B. Stonehouse, F. F. Bruce, and Gordon D. Fee (Grand Rapids: Eerdmans Publishing, 2014), III, A, 3, C, Olive Tree Bible Software.

from that of a pagan husband that a 'mixed' marriage, where the 'two become one,' is simply unthinkable."[16] Therefore, from Fee's point of view, a clash of perspectives and value systems is the reason for Paul's proviso. I would disagree on Fee's point that Paul's use of μόνον ἐν κυρίῳ is written out of "good sense" rather than a command. For Fee to make such an inference is to ignore the many injunctions in the Old Testament that speak authoritatively on this matter and indeed, Fee makes no reference to Old Testament passages on this matter. I can understand why one could refer to it as mere "good sense" as opposed to firm instruction. Fee fails to colligate a whole body of commands concerning interfaith marriage in the Old Testament. These are passages with which Paul undoubtedly was thoroughly familiar with as a Jew. A better analysis is purported by David Garland's commentary on this subject, for he does take into account the Old Testament prohibitions.

> If Paul expects widows to marry only Christians, it would fit the endogamous mores of the OT and Jewish tradition (cf. Deut. 7:3; Josh. 23:12; Neh. 13:23–25; Tob. 4:12–13; Jos. As. 8:5–7; T. Levi 9:10; m. Giṭ. 9:2; b. Qidd. 70b), which were so much a part of his background (see also Instone-Brewer 2001: 237–38). Paul had few other ways of expressing the concept "Christian" (cf. Acts 11:26; 26:28; 1 Pet. 4:16), and his greeting to "those in the Lord who belong to the family of Narcissus" (Rom. 16:11) shows that he can use the phrase ἐν κυρίῳ (en kyriō) to mean "Christians."[17]

---

[16] Fee, *Corinthians*, III, A, 3, C.

[17] David E. Garland, *1 Corinthians*, Baker Exegetical Commentary on the New Testament, eds. Robert W. Yarbrough and Joshua W. Jipp (Grand Rapids: Baker Academic, 2003), 344.

Joseph Fitzmyer also makes reference to the Old Testament prohibitions:

> This nuance is new, in that Paul prefers that she marry a Christian, which is a counsel against entering into a mixed marriage. Paul is undoubtedly extending a Jewish notion, expressed in such OT endogamic regulations as Deut 7:3; Ezra 9:2; 11QTemple a (11Q19) 57:19 ("from his father's house and from his family"), to the Christians of Corinth.[18]

As much as I applaud Fitzmyer's inclusion of Old Testament references to this matter (and he even uses the term "undoubtedly" to highlight the certainty of influence it had on Paul's use of μόνον ἐν κυρίῳ), it is unfortunate that Fitzmyer uses the word "prefers" which softens the instruction. Equally unfortunate is how he refers to these Old Testament endogamic regulations as mere "Jewish notion." When one examines all the relevant Old Testament references concerning interfaith marriages, it is clear that God's command to only marry within the covenant community is by no means a divine suggestion born out of "good sense" nor a mere preference, but a firm and forceful divine stance against the wiles of idolatry. **Thus, if we do recognise Paul's μόνον ἐν κυρίῳ as having been written "undoubtedly" as an extension of Old Testament endogamic regulations, then one must also carry over the firmness of the prohibitive stance and term Paul's μόνον ἐν κυρίῳ as an instruction or command to be obeyed by the covenant community of the New Testament.**

---

[18] Joseph A. Fitzmyer, *First Corinthians*, The Anchor Yale Bible Commentaries, ed. John J. Collins (New Haven: Yale University Press, 2008), 329.

4

IS IT A SIN?

Having this μόνον ἐν κυρίῳ instruction/command in the New Testament gives us the confidence to believe that the Old Testament prohibition on interfaith marriages still stands, even today. **In contrast, one will be hard-pressed to find a single verse in the New Testament that even remotely suggests that the interfaith marriage prohibition had been lifted.** Therefore, to disregard this prohibition today is to disobey Scripture, and hence, interfaith marriage in today's context should rightly be understood as a sin. In dealing with the subject of freedom in Christ, Paul concludes the matter by stating a timeless, universal principle that defines for us what sin is in Rom. 14:23b: "For whatever does not proceed from faith is sin." To be doing anything that proceeds from faith in God is to trust in God and do the things that testify of his trustworthiness and in so doing, God is glorified. Therefore, the essence of sin is the opposite of doing deeds that exhibit trust in God. Colin Kruse views Rom. 14:23b as a "humble reliance on God, on God alone, for salvation and for the living out of the implications of that salvation. What cannot be justified by being in accord with our relation to Christ is sin" and that "the believer who sometimes does things that are not motivated by faith. It is those things that have the nature of sin."[19]

In light of this definition of sin, it becomes increasingly clear that getting entangled in an unequally yoked romantic relationship is a sin, since it cannot be said to have been motivated by faith. In fact, it is termed as having "broken faith" in Ezra 10:2. It is a clear projection of trust issues with God. Unless the Christian has absolutely no idea of what God's Word says of such relationships, to forge ahead with an interfaith marriage should rightly be considered a faithless act, done out of a lack of trust in God's goodness in setting boundaries for his people. Such lack of trust leading to disobedience to God's instructions is sin. If whatever that is done without accompanying faith is sin, then indeed, it is not difficult to fall into sin. Even good deeds done out of a cowardly sense of human insecurity are sin, since trust in God is absent in the doing of these outwardly noble deeds. It is a sobering and humbling thought to know that it does not take much for us to fall into sin.

Such thinking is good in the sense that it translates to a high view of God's commands and holy standards. The more we get acquainted with God's holiness, the more we realize the ease with which sin emerges within us. In some countries, the consumption of marijuana for recreation is lawful. So, if a Christian consumes such drugs in those countries, would that be a sin? The fact is, nowhere in the Bible does it state that God's people must stay away from recreational drugs. Yet there are enough principles and clues

---

[19] Colin G. Kruse, *Paul's Letter to the Romans*, The Pillar New Testament Commentary, ed. D. A. Carson (Grand Rapids: Eerdmans Publishing, 2012), VI, G, Olive Tree Bible Software.

in the Scripture for us to confidently deem it a sin. **In the case of unequally yoked romantic relationships, we have much more than principles and clues to work with.** We can with confidence say interfaith marriage is a sin.

The teaching on marriage and dating must go hand in hand. Once we have established that interfaith marriage is disobedience to Scripture, we must then begin to see its connection with dating, since dating for the Christian is essentially, as Tim Clinton and Chap Clark put it, a "precursor to marriage." They go on to say:

> Dating someone who is serious about his faith is a clear biblical command for the Christian. Even if the individual claims to be a Christian, it is important to evaluate his level of spiritual maturity as an important factor in determining compatibility. To have a godly relationship, it is critical for both partners to be able to encourage and build up one another in faith.[20]

Therefore, if dating is regarded as a precursor to marriage, then to be in a dating relationship with an unbeliever is a sin too, since one has placed oneself on the very path that leads toward sin. To knowingly head toward sin certainly demonstrates a lack of faith in the goodness of God.

To condemn unequally yoked relationships as sin can come across as harsh and uncompassionate. The alternative is to sugarcoat the truth. Imagine offering counsel to a young adult who has fallen deeply in love with an unbeliever and calling their potential union "not out of good sense" or "biblically inadvisable." It will be an almost impossible task to convince this young adult

---

[20] Tim Clinton and Chap Clark, *The Quick-Reference Guide to Counseling Teenagers* (Grand Rapids: Baker Books, 2010) 107.

who is experiencing the euphoria of romance to take a second look at his or her choices by appealing to his or her "good sense." At some point, this young adult will ask the pointed question, "Is it a sin?" How a minister answers that question will lead this young adult to very different life trajectories. **When we fail to call a spade a spade, we do these young people no favors.** These are singles with a good chance of avoiding this pitfall if we would only arm them with the unadulterated truth right from the start.

Yet, having said that, there is another category of believers with whom we must exercise an extra measure of compassion and graciousness. These are those who have already gotten into an unequally yoked marriage. **These are the ones we show gentleness to and pray that they find unconditional acceptance in the community life of the church.** Even though we do not compromise the truth with them (for they too need to be armed with the truth in order to influence the next generation rightly), it is our desire to journey pastorally with such marriages in the hope that the unbelieving spouse will one day come to faith and new life in Christ. Therefore, we do well to befriend their non-Christian spouses and approach the subject with them gently and with great patience. In contrast, when speaking about this subject to Christian singles who still have the potential for a Christian marriage, we want to be firm and forceful, clear and direct with the truth. Therefore, this is the tension a wise minister must maintain.

In dealing with this unequally yoked subject, especially in addressing singles, one needs to be clear that the biblical theology of interfaith marriages does point to it being a sin; from Old Testament to New Testament, it is a sin. Christian singles who choose to marry outside of the covenant community are being disobedient to Scripture. However, the same cannot and must not be said of Christians and non-Christians who are already in a marriage relationship, where both were not Christians when the marriage took place. In fact, Paul demonstrates support for such marriages (1 Cor. 7:12-16).[21] In such situations, Paul tells them not to divorce, perhaps in case they have the mistaken belief that a Christian ought to, by default, forsake such an unideal union, given such strong prohibition of interfaith marriages taught in Old Testament Scriptures. Therefore, one ought to be clear that it is not wrong if both parties in a marriage are not God's people when they got married, but along the way, one partner converts. So the discussion in this book is specifically referring to interfaith marriages which came about as a result of willful disobedience to God before the marriage takes place and not after.

---

[21] Daniel Berchie, "Marrying an 'Unbelieving' Partner: An Exegetical Study of 2 Corinthians 6:14," *Valley View University Journal of Theology* 3 (2014): 76.

PART 2

God's Ideal for Spiritually Healthy Marriages

5

THE PRIORITY
OF SPIRITUAL
COMPATIBILITY

Genesis 24 records for us the most elaborate account of an arranged marriage. It is the longest chapter in Genesis. One would expect the lengthiest treatment in Genesis to be about the creation of the world or perhaps Abraham's covenant with God, but that honor went to the subject of marriage.[22] As Abraham sought the help of his most senior servant to arrange an ideal marriage for his son, Isaac, it is noteworthy that the very first thing he did was to make his servant swear that he will not take a wife for his son from among the Canaanites (v. 3). Since Abraham had already left his home country, Haran, and is now dwelling in Canaan, the most convenient marriage option would be to arrange a marriage between Isaac and a pagan Canaanite woman. To make

---

[22] Victor P. Hamilton, *The Book of Genesis: Chapters 18-50,* New International Commentary on the Old Testament, ed. Robert L. Hubbard (Grand Rapids: Eerdmans Publishing, 1990), II, M, 1, Olive Tree Bible Software.

that long trip back to Abraham's birth country would be the least favorable option unless Abraham had other priorities in mind. Victor Hamilton claims that

> Abraham does not instruct his servant to select a bride who believes in Yahweh. Religious qualifications of the bride or her family are not part of the agreement. Later chapters reveal that Laban, Rebekah's brother, was a practicing polytheist, who panicked when "his gods" were stolen. The concern is that Isaac's future wife be Aramean and not Canaanite… Isaac must avoid a local intermarriage and emigration to the land of his father. If Isaac is to inherit the land, he must not marry among those destined to disinherit the land. [23]

I differ from Hamilton's point that Abraham's priority was for Isaac not to marry those "destined to disinherit the land." This is because if that is so, then a bride from any other surrounding lands (as long as the bride is not from Canaan) would have sufficed. For Abraham to specifically pinpoint his birth country is telling that he is familiar with the culture and spiritual practices there and saw it as the most aligned to the worship of Yahweh and therefore a bride from Haran would have been a spiritually superior choice as compared to a bride from Canaan. In other words, Hamilton's argument is that Abraham's choice of Haran rather than Canaan was on the basis of avoiding obtaining a bride from a people that would never inherit the land while I would argue that Abraham's choice of Haran was a matter of prioritizing spiritual compatibility. No doubt, idolatry may have crept in as Hamilton notes in the case of Rebekah's brother, yet getting a bride for Isaac from his own people would have been the most spiritually compatible option

---

[23] Hamilton, *Genesis*, II, M, 1.

compared to other nations to the best of his knowledge. John Goldingay observes that even though idolatry existed in Abraham's birth country, the servant's interaction with Laban (Rebekah's brother) and Bethuel (Rebekah's father) supports the idea that a bride from Abraham's birth country is the most spiritually viable option.

> They surely served other deities; Yahweh had not been involved with them. But the ease with which not only the servant speaks of Yahweh before them (vv. 35, 40, 42, 44, 48, and 56) but they also speak of Yahweh to him (vv. 31, 50, and 51) suggests that the story's perspective is that Abraham need not worry about religious contamination from a wife with that background.[24]

With this spiritually positive dialogue in mind, we can understand Abraham's insistence on Isaac's bride being from his own relatives even to the point of having his servant swear by the Lord. Goldingay also noted that this account of a bride for Isaac "fits an emphasis in both Testaments that the people of God should marry within the "family" (see, e.g., Ezra 9:1–2; 2 Cor. 6:14–18)."[25] Kenneth Mathews asserts that "only one family therefore can confidently qualify, the Nahor branch of his father's lineage (v.4),"[26] linking the discussion to how the "Mosaic legislation prohibits intermarriage with groups outside the covenant nation, leading to religious apostasy."[27] **Therefore, it stands to reason that this story acts as an apt paradigm for God's people to make**

---

[24] John Goldingay, *Genesis*, Baker Commentary on the Old Testament: Pentateuch, ed. Bill Arnold (Grand Rapids: Baker Academic, 2020), 377.

[25] Goldingay, *Genesis*, 376.

[26] Kenneth A. Mathews, *Genesis 11:27-50:26*, The New American Commentary, ed. E. Ray Clendenen (Nashville: Broadman & Holman Publishers, 2005), 327.

[27] Mathews, *Genesis*, 326-27.

spiritual compatibility the priority in attaining a spiritually healthy marriage. For Abraham, even though the journey is long, a bride from his own home country is the only acceptable option since it is the most tenable in terms of spiritual compatibility. For God's people today, if a believer is to prioritize spiritual compatibility just as Abraham did, then the only acceptable option would be marriage with a fellow believer as spelled out by New Testament standards to which we shall now turn.

6

PURSUING THAT IDEAL PICTURE

In Eph. 5:22-33, the apostle Paul offers us a paradigm for marriage. After he makes the case for the gender roles of headship and submission within a marriage, he goes on to establish the foundational truth that undergirds his instructions. Verse 31 bears this foundational statement which is a quote that hails back to Gen. 2:24: "Therefore a man shall leave his father and his mother and hold fast to his wife, and they shall become one flesh." The next verse speaks of a mystery that is only revealed in this new covenant age. This mystery that Paul speaks of is that this foundational statement "refers to Christ and the church" (v. 32). In other words, the divine goal of marriage is ultimately to be a showcase for the covenant love between Christ and the church.

The marriage union is meant to reflect the relationship between Christ and the church. This is what Paul calls the "profound" meaning of marriage. A marriage between a man and a woman is made in the very image of Christ's marriage with the church. Out of this beautiful mystery come the fundamental roles of husbands and wives. In verses 22-24, Paul instructs wives to submit to their husbands in the same way the church would submit to Jesus "in everything." In verses 25-30, Paul then turns to the husbands and instructs them to love their wives just as Christ loves the church, even to the point of giving up his life for her. Therefore, in order for this image of marriage to be as true to the picture of Christ and the church as possible, both husbands and wives must be constantly looking to the godly relational dynamics between Christ and the church in order to effectively fulfill their respective gender roles within their marriages. This is no walk in the park, as many Christian couples attest. As sinners, we constantly struggle in fulfilling the roles laid out in this portion of Scripture. However, as with the many instructions in Paul's letters, they offer us an ideal to strive toward and so we do not give up; we die to self and press on, for this is the ideal picture of marriage that God expects us to pattern after–a pattern rooted in Christ's marriage to the church and thus a pattern for "every age and all cultures."[28]

If Christ's relationship with the church is the ideal picture of marriage that God has given for all marriages to pattern after, then it stands to reason that an unequally yoked marriage will not be able to strive toward such a picture. At best, we will have the believer in the marriage drawing strength and wisdom from God to fulfill his or her God-given role in the marriage. In contrast, the unbeliever in the marriage will not wish to, or will have no access to the spiritual resources needed to pattern his or her part after that ideal picture. Lisa Baumert observes Paul's instructions to husbands and wives as part of a larger framework in which Paul

---

[28] Christopher Ash, *Married for God: Making Your Marriage the Best It Can Be* (Nottingham: IVP, 2007), 86.

also addresses slaves and masters, children and fathers. She affirms that Paul's call to "be filled with the Spirit" in Eph 5:18 ought to be "the interpretative key" in unlocking these three relationships, and therefore it is the indwelling of the Holy Spirit that enables Christians to live out the ideals pointed out by Paul pertaining to the three relationships.[29] **Hence, one cannot expect an unbeliever without the indwelling of the Spirit to appreciate the glorious meaning that God has assigned to marriage, much less expect the unbeliever to pursue this spiritual cause of reflecting Christ and the church.** To the world, marriage has a myriad of meanings, and Christ and the church would be furthest from their thoughts, and understandably so. Unbelievers may also disagree on the gender roles instructed by Paul and dismiss them as backward in the midst of a progressive age.

In his book, *The Meaning of Marriage*, Timothy Keller notes that "if God had the gospel of Jesus's salvation in mind when he established marriage, then marriage only 'works' to the degree that it approximates the pattern of God's self-giving love in Christ."[30] However, one could argue that many marriages between non-Christians, and even unequally yoked marriages "work" too. That is, non-Christian or unequally yoked marriages can also achieve great success in faithfulness and harmony. The problem with such marriages is that they are not driven by "God's self-giving love in Christ," and therefore will always fall short of God's ideal for a

---

[29] Lisa Baumert, "Biblical Interpretation and the Epistle to the Ephesians," *Priscilla Papers* 31, no. 4 (Fall 2017): 30.

[30] Timothy Keller, *The Meaning of Marriage: Facing the Complexities of Commitment with the Wisdom of God* (London: Hodder and Stoughton, 2011), 46.

spiritually healthy marriage. Keller spells out the pitfalls of unequally yoked marriages in another part of his book.

> If you do marry someone who does not share your faith, then there are only two ways to proceed. One is that you will more and more have to lose your transparency. In the normal, healthy Christian life, you relate Christ and the gospel to everything. You will think of Christ when watching a movie. You will think about what you read in the Bible that day. But if you are natural and transparent about all of these thoughts, your partner will find it at least tedious or annoying and even offensive. He or she will say, "I had no idea you were this overboard about your faith." You will just have to hide it all.
>
> The other, worse possibility is that you move Christ out of a central place in your consciousness. You will have to let your heart's ardor for Christ cool. You will have to deliberately not think out how your Christian commitment relates to every area of your life. You will demote Christ in your mind and heart, because if you keep him central, you will feel isolated from your spouse.
>
> Both of these possible outcomes, are of course, terrible. That is why you should not deliberately marry someone who does not share your Christian faith.[31]

As Keller so aptly points out, the spiritual health of an unequally yoked marriage will inevitably suffer one way or the other.

The husband-and-wife relationship is like no other human relationship. The marriage relationship between a man and a woman is the closest, most intimate relationship characterized by a lifelong covenantal commitment. Yet with such closeness and extended tenure come the inevitable conflicts that must surely

---

[31] Keller, *Meaning*, 210-11.

occur between two imperfect and sinful beings. Despite the harsh realities of life that marriage often wakes people up to, Ephesians 5 shows us that God is glorified. The relationship between Christ and the church is exemplified when a husband and a wife persevere in faithfulness and forgiveness through humble dependence on Christ and deliberate obedience to his ways. Such devotion and reliance can only happen when both the husband and wife in the marriage are believers. It is only in equally yoked marriages that it is possible to find both partners in unison, aspiring toward the glorious picture of Christ and the church. An equally yoked marriage is at the least, the starting place to achieve God's ideal for spiritually healthy marriages.

PART 3

The Key to Joy and Fulfilment

7
THE POWER OF RELATIONSHIPS

When a Christian is tempted by the prospect of starting a romantic relationship with a non-Christian, even though he or she may be familiar with the biblical prohibitions that stretch from the Old Testament to the New Testament, he or she may still ask, "Why should I obey God's Word on this subject?" He or she may entertain the thought that perhaps one might be better off and be able to live a more joyful and fulfilling life if one were to disobey God's Word on this matter and enter into an unequally yoked relationship. Joy and fulfilment in their earthly lives may be their priority in the here and now. Yet it is precisely for our joy and fulfilment, both in this age and the age to come, that God's Word offers to all who would heed it by faith.

Relationships are powerful. Being entangled in the wrong relationship can lead one astray and toward destruction, while right relationships can lead to joy and fulfilment. One of the clearest warnings we have from the New Testament concerning the power of relationships is found in 2 Cor. 6:14: "Do not be unequally yoked with unbelievers. For what partnership has righteousness with lawlessness? Or what fellowship has light with darkness?" This is no doubt a call to the Corinthians to distance themselves from unbelievers. To be sure, 1 Cor. 5:10, which acknowledges reasonable connection with unbelievers as unavoidable (if one were to be living in this world), rules out the possibility of Paul asking the Corinthians to cease all contact with unbelievers.[32]

David Starling views ἄπιστοι, (being translated as "unbelievers") as the "idol-worshipping pagans of Corinth" and more specifically, Paul's opponents or false teachers that Paul is dealing with. He observes that the flow from Paul's complaint of lack of affection (6:11-13; 7:2-3) to competing affection for false teachers (6:14–7:1) fits the narrative that ἄπιστοι refers to the competing false teachers which also belong to the unbelieving category.[33] Therefore, it behooves one to be clear on the original context of 2 Cor. 6:14 before applying its prohibition on other contexts.

Although this verse is often used to disapprove of interfaith marriages, admittedly, the immediate context of this passage is not talking about marriages at all. In studying the context of the passage, William Web notes the implausible nature of linking 6:14 to interfaith marriages, or in his terms, mixed marriages, in its original context:

---

[32] Donald G. McDougall, "Unequally Yoked–a Re-Examination of 2 Corinthians 6:11-7:4," *The Master's Seminary Journal* 10, no. 1 (Spr 1999): 132.

[33] David Ian Starling, "The Ἄπιστοι of 2 Cor 6:14: Beyond the Impasse," *Novum Testamentum* 55, no. 1 (2013): 51.

> Also it is improbable that Paul had mixed marriages in mind. Mixed marriages, while metonymical idolatry of a sort, are an unsuitable referent in light of the actual (not simply potential) nature of the problem in the passage, the Old Testament imperatives, the immediate nature of the idolatry, the broad audience, no mention of idolatry in relation to the mixed marriage earlier, and this not being an area of intense personal conflict between the apostle and the Corinthians.[34]

The improbability of the context being interfaith marriages becomes evident as we examine the preceding verse (13): "In return (I speak as to children) widen your hearts also." In verse 13, we find Paul pleading with the Corinthians to open their hearts to him, because he is trying to convince them that he is indeed a true apostle of Jesus Christ. On the one hand, Paul urges them to open their hearts to him, and on the other hand, he pleads with the Corinthians not to open their hearts to false teachers who are leading them toward idolatry. Therefore, it is in such a false teacher and idolatry context that Paul warns them not to be unequally yoked with them.[35] In using the term "unequally yoked," Paul is saying that the person whom you open your heart to, will shape your values and beliefs. At the heart of this verse is ἑτεροζυγοῦντες where we get the term "unequally yoked" as translated in the King James Bible. Murray Harris in his study of the word notes:

> The verb ἑτεροζυγέω is not found elsewhere in Biblical Greek nor in Greek literature before the Christian era. Literally it means "pull

---

[34] William J. Webb, "Unequally Yoked Together with Unbelievers," *Bibliotheca Sacra* 149, no. 594 (April 1992): 179.

[35] Paul Barnett, *The Second Epistle to the Corinthians,* New International Commentary on the New Testament, eds. Ned B. Stonehouse, F. F. Bruce, and Gordon D. Fee (Grand Rapids: Eerdmans Publishing, 1997), III, D, 6, b, Olive Tree Bible Software.

the yoke [ζυγός] in a different [ἕτερος] direction than one's fellow," and figuratively, "make a mismatched covenant," "mismate" (Spicq 2.80). In this periphrastic construction, then, it means "be yoked in unequal partnership" (LSJ 701 s.v.), with the second element (-ζυγέω) "governing" the first (ἑτερο-) (BDF §119(1)). When the cognate adjective ἑτερόζυγος, "unevenly yoked," "yoked to a stronger," is used substantively (as in Lev. 19:19), it refers to an animal of a different kind. This OT passage prohibits the cross-breeding of animals. "You shall not mate different kinds of animals" (Lev. 19:19), which the LXX renders "You shall not breed your cattle with an animal that uses another yoke (ἑτεροζύγῳ . . ." Similarly, Deut. 22:9-11 prohibits a mixing of diverse elements: two different kinds of animals in ploughing ("Do not plough with an ox and a donkey yoked together," 22:10 [LXX has simply ἐπὶ τὸ αὐτό, "together"]), two different kinds of seeds in sowing (22:9), and two different kinds of yarn in making textiles (22:11). In alluding to Lev. 19:19 and Dt. 22:10 by the use of the verb ἑτεροζυγέω, Paul is saying that just as the yoking together of animals of two disparate species to form a team will result in an incongruous mismatch, so close attachments and intimate association between believers and unbelievers will produce an ill-matched union and total dissonance.[36]

Therefore, if Harris is correct in identifying Paul's use of ἑτεροζυγοῦντες as an allusion to Lev. 19:19 and Deut. 22:10, then the picture that Paul is presenting to the Corinthians is that of different animals (an ox and a donkey) being yoked together, working the field together where both will "pull the yoke in a different direction" due to the mismatch, causing dissonance and

---

[36] Murray J. Harris, *The Second Epistle to the Corinthians*, The New International Greek Testament Commentary, ed. Mark Goodacre and Todd D. Still (Grand Rapids: Eerdmans Publishing, 2013), I, C, 4, b, Olive Tree Bible Software.

much frustration but yet eventually, both will head toward the same direction since they are yoked together. In other words, Corinthians who choose to maintain close relationships with the false teachers will eventually walk in unison with them despite the internal conflicts between the faith and practice of believers and the false teachers. Whether in thought or deed, eventually, the false teachers will be very influential in steering the direction of the lives of the Corinthian believers. Such "fleshly" influence will steer the Corinthian believers toward distorted assessments of Paul and render them captive to the pagan mindset of the surrounding culture.[37] It is no wonder then that Paul persuades the Corinthians to open their hearts to himself (or be yoked with Paul himself) and not to the false teachers.

However, just because the text is not specifically addressing the context of dating and marriage does not mean that one cannot take the unequally yoked principle and apply it to other contexts like dating, marriage, or even business partnerships. Paul's appeal may entail broader applications for the Corinthians to be mindful to avoid any public or private relationship with unbelievers that could potentially compromise Christian standards.[38] Through 2 Cor. 6:14, we see the truth of this principle: whomever you open your heart to, that person will greatly influence your faith and spirituality. Essentially, you will be like that person; you will take on his or her beliefs and outlook in life. This is what the Corinthians are in danger of in having close fellowship with the false teachers.

---

[37] Starling, "Ἄπιστοι," 60.

[38] Harris, *Second Corinthians*, I, C, 4, b.

Applying the unequally yoked principle to marriage, we can see the love of God in desiring what is best–what is most joyous and fulfilling for his children. As marriage partners "open their hearts to each other" like an ox and a donkey yoked together, an unequally yoked marriage will inevitably have clashes in worldview, lifestyle, and priorities. This would have an impact on decision-making on many levels. Things get even more complicated when children enter into the picture. **The unequally yoked principle makes the implication that the believer will be drawn into a slippery slope where he or she becomes more and more in step with the unbeliever, much like the golden chain of events spelled out in Deut. 7:3-4.** A lifetime of split loyalties is not an equation leading to joy and fulfilment.

8
INTERPRETING OUR OBSERVATIONS RIGHTLY

Would it be possible for the believer to be the one to lead the unbeliever toward the path of righteousness? In the unequally yoked passage, Paul did not entertain such an option. No hints were given with regard to the possibility of the Corinthians influencing the false teachers toward the truth. Paul's message was simply to steer clear of the false teachers. His utmost concern is for his flock to not fall prey to idolatry. However, one can certainly argue by means of empirical data in our day and age, that there are cases where a believer, having persisted in marriage with an unbeliever, manages to maintain his or her Christian witness and remain faithful in devotion and service unto the Lord, and thus it would appear that he or she was well able to circumvent the lure of idolatry despite having entered an unequally yoked marriage. Yet one must also see that such observations are subjective. This is because idolatry exists in various forms.

Colossians 3:5 states: "Put to death therefore what is earthly in you: sexual immorality, impurity, passion, evil desire, and covetousness, which is idolatry." Besides bowing down to false deities, such worldly influences are also deemed idolatrous according to God's Word. Perhaps without the worldly influence of an unbelieving spouse, the said believer would have possessed a much greater measure of spirituality and fervency in gospel work. **Therefore, it is impossible to say for sure, simply through personal observation, that the presence of an unbelieving spouse had failed to steer a believer toward the path of idolatry in an unequally yoked marriage.**

There is also the oft-cited evidence of so-called "success stories" where a non-Christian in an unequally yoked dating or marriage relationship eventually converts and even becomes an effective evangelist for the Lord. How does one explain such phenomena? Lee and Leslie Strobel, in their book, *Spiritual Mismatch*, share their wisdom on this:

> Resist the temptation to do missionary dating. The problem with stories about Christians dating unbelievers and then leading them to Christ is that they are the exception to the rule. The chances are far higher that you will be pulled away from your faith than he or she will embrace what you believe. Remember that it is wrong to knowingly violate God's injunction against unequally yoked relationships. While it is natural and healthy to be concerned about the salvation of a potential dating partner, the best approach is to connect him with a member of the same sex to talk about the gospel, give him a Christian book to read, invite him to your

church or Christian youth group, and pray for him. You can take all those positive steps without putting yourself in harm's way.[39]

"Success stories" of such nature, whether it be in dating or marriage, ought to be regarded as exceptions rather than the norm. Such cases should rightly be seen as acts of God's generous grace. **Nevertheless, our responsibility as Christians is not to presume upon God's grace and act on the possibility of what God may do, but to act on what God has already told us in his Word.** As followers of Christ, we are called to do what God has instructed us to do rather than disobeying his instructions by presuming upon his grace. One must be careful to avoid justifying an unbiblical act just because there are cases where something good came out of such acts. For example, the biblical story of Joseph can be seen as a story with a glorious salvific outcome. However, such a grandly positive outcome would never have occurred if not for the evil plotting of Joseph's brothers. His brothers intended evil, but God used that very act of cruelty to set in motion a chain of events that would lead to God's people being saved from famine (Gen. 50:20). Yet God's act of grace in this instance in no way justifies the victimization of helpless siblings. One does not take (albeit) positive outcomes we observe in life to overthrow the timeless boundaries that God in his goodness has set for his people. "When the Bible tells us 'Do not be yoked together with unbelievers' (2 Corinthians 6:14), the intent is to protect Christians from relationships where their faith can be compromised."[40] God's

---

[39] Lee Strobel and Leslie Strobel, *Spiritual Mismatch: Hope for Christians Married to Someone Who Doesn't Know God* (Grand Rapids: Zondervan, 2017), 203.
[40] Strobel and Strobel, *Spiritual Mismatch*, 189.

boundaries are there to prevent his people from putting their faith at risk.

9

TRUSTING GOD'S GOODNESS, HEEDING GOD'S INSTRUCTIONS

As beings made in the image of God, we find true joy and fulfilment only as we reflect God in us. If being Christ-like is the goal of every Christian, then entering what might be the closest relationship in our lifetime with an unbeliever, is to knowingly make it more challenging to strive toward this goal of Christ-likeness. This derailing of our bid for Christ-likeness must be recognized in its very essence as idolatrous. Elsewhere, in 1 Cor. 15:33, Paul says, "Do not be deceived: 'Bad company ruins good morals.'" Whom we choose to have close relationships with will have an impact on our pilgrimage toward Christ-like character. In the study of this verse, Roy Ciampa and Brian Rosner note:

> The point is to be aware (and beware) of the corrupting influence that comes from extended intimate fellowship with others and to

take steps to make sure 1) we are spending sufficient time in extended intimate fellowship with people who know and love God and who are known by him; and that 2) in our relationships with those who do not yet know Christ we are being a positive influence as salt and light in their midst (Matt. 5:13-16). It is of utmost importance to guard our hearts and the influences upon our moral compass. As we have argued throughout this commentary (as have others) some Corinthians were being overly influenced by the dominant values and thinking of the Corinthian city and of Roman culture and insufficiently influenced by their knowledge of Christ and of the basic moral and theological teachings of the Christian faith. They needed to learn how to be in the world without acting as people who were of the world. [41]

Marriage would most certainly qualify as "extended intimate fellowship" and therefore to marry an unbeliever, one would have failed in guarding one's heart, allowing for corrupting influences upon one's moral compass. It is true then that this unequally yoked principle can be applied to all sorts of relationships, but it is especially relevant to the marriage relationship, since that is the most intimate of relationships and meant to be the most permanent of relationships. If God saw fit to place the unequally yoked principle in the Scriptures, then we do well to trust that heeding it will only lead to our good, as we believe in a God who works all things in our best interest as a loving Father would.

There are many instructions in the Bible where God does not reveal why those instructions should be kept. The rationale behind those instructions was never explained. For example, under

---

[41] Roy E. Ciampa and Brian S. Rosner, *The First Letter to the Corinthians*, The Pillar New Testament Commentary, ed. D.A. Carson (Grand Rapids: Eerdmans Publishing, 2010), V, D, Olive Tree Bible Software.

Moses's law, God's people are instructed to break any earthenware vessel if they happen to find any dead lizard in it (Lev. 11:29-33). Other than calling the situation unclean, no other explanation was given to logically persuade the Israelites to comply with the instruction. One would imagine that some commentary on hygiene would have been more persuasive. The people of God are simply expected to trust and obey. The goodness of God as seen in how God freed them–how he bore them up on eagle's wings, rescuing them out of the scourge of Egypt–is reason enough for these freed people to heed every instruction of God, whether or not they are explained.[42] Indeed, God's people are often exhorted to trust in the Lord wholeheartedly; to not depend on their own human wisdom. To do so will lead to human flourishing (success). This is precisely what is spelled out in Prov. 3:5-6: "Trust in the Lord with all your heart, and do not lean on your own understanding. In all your ways acknowledge him, and he will make straight your paths." The Hebrew word "yasar" being translated as "straight" in this verse speaks of "smoothness" of the path taken, denoting God-given success in an undertaking.[43] The prime example of this mindset is Abraham's obedience in his willingness to offer up Isaac. Abraham is expected to obey God's instructions to sacrifice his son simply based on his understanding of God's character and trust that obedience to this good God can only lead to the ultimate good. This is to be the kind of mind that should characterize God's people–a mindset that is willing to heed

---

[42] Patrick D. Miller, "Divine Command/Divine Law: A Biblical Perspective," *Studies in Christian Ethics* 23, no. 1 (February 2010): 33.

[43] Bruce K. Waltke, *The Book of Proverbs: Chapters 1-15*, New International Commentary on the Old Testament, ed. Robert L. Hubbard (Grand Rapids: Eerdmans Publishing, 2004), I, B, 4a, Olive Tree Bible Software.

God's instructions even when they do not fully understand the nuts and bolts concerning the instruction; a mindset that possesses the full assurance that in obeying God, joy and fulfilment will surely follow. In fact, Christians may not even need to hear a specific command from God before acting in ways pleasing to him. The Bible teaches us to act based on our understanding of God and his ways. Benjamin Scolnic makes a good observation on this matter in his discussion of Abraham's obedience in sacrificing Isaac.

> Even though God did not explicitly say, "Do not take another wife/surrogate/ concubine," God thought that it was clear that God, and only God, would give Abraham his true link to his descendants. God can be displeased with certain acts even when God did not issue a command or express displeasure at the possible act. God does not say, "Do not go to the other side of the Jabbok" but takes action when Jacob does. God does not tell Moses, "Do not hit the rock" but God is disappointed and angry that Moses does not just speak to the rock (Num. 20). And so in the Akedah, God's command and promise was: I will make of you a great nation (Gen. 12:1); I will make your offspring as the dust of the earth (Gen. 13:16); . . . for I make you the father of a multitude of nations. I will make you exceedingly fertile (17:5-6). It is correct to say that God does not say: "Do not go have a baby any way that you like. Do not go get a surrogate or another wife or a concubine." But God does say: "I will give you a child." In all of these verses, the emphasis should be on the "I."[44]

It is thus clear that God can be displeased with the actions of his people even when he has not given explicit instructions on the

---

[44] Benjamin Edidin Scolnic, "Master of Life: Why God Commands Abraham to Sacrifice Isaac (Gen. 22)," *Jewish Bible Quarterly* 48, no. 3 (July 2020): 192.

matter. Christians in an unequally yoked dating relationship oftentimes take comfort in the fact that an overtly clear and explicit "thou shall not" commandment has not been issued in the New Testament. However, such statements are not a strict necessity to decipher God's will. Drawing from the many accounts of God's dealings with interfaith marriages and their propensity to lead one toward idolatry, one can easily discern God's heart on this matter. Christians cannot claim to be living a life of joy and fulfilment if they are knowingly in rebellion against God's wishes.

First Peter 3:7 embodies this principle of trusting God even when we do not fully understand: "Likewise, husbands, live with your wives in an understanding way, showing honor to the woman as the weaker vessel, since they are heirs with you of the grace of life, so that your prayers may not be hindered." This verse is significant to our discussion because it shows that God cares about our married life; that God knows what we must do in a marriage that would lead to human flourishing and in this instance, specifically, the flourishing of our prayer life. During biblical times, it is a common societal tendency for husbands to dominate and exploit their wives since they are the "weaker vessel." Peter warns against it, not with logical consequences like strained relationships between husbands and wives but with consequences of a divine nature.[45] There is no explanation as to how failure to show honor to wives will lead to hindered prayers. What is implied here is a correlation between a husband's relationship with his wife and his relationship with God. Why does such a correlation exist? Why did

---

[45] Peter H. Davids, *The First Epistle of Peter,* New International Commentary on the Old Testament, ed. Robert L. Hubbard (Grand Rapids: Eerdmans Publishing, 1990), III, D. Olive Tree Bible Software.

God cause such a correlation to exist? The Scripture, in this instance, did not connect the dots for us, even though calculated guesses can be made. How do husbands not treating their wives rightly, create blockages to their prayers? We are simply told that it does, and husbands do well to evaluate how they have been treating their wives if they were to face a season of unanswered prayers.

God's people must heed God's instructions even when they are not told the rationale behind the instructions. Moreover, the call to avoid interfaith marriages is not one of those instructions with unknown rationales. God has clearly spoken in Exod. 34:11-17 and Deut. 7:3-4 that the reason for the prohibition is idolatry. The Bible has consistently attested that God's people who have been drawn into the fleeting pleasures of idolatry always eventually end up in a place of failure and regret. Idolatry has never led a single one of God's people to lasting joy and fulfilment.

10
ON GOD'S TERMS, NOT OURS

At the end of the day, one has to understand joy and fulfilment on God's terms and not our own. If a Christian thinks that in rejecting the advances of a non-Christian, he or she will ultimately be rewarded with someone better–somebody who is a Christian–and then be able to live happily ever after, then such a person is leaning upon his or her own definition of joy and fulfilment which may or may not be in alignment with God's plan for the person. In reality, a Christian who rejects the advances of an unbeliever may very well end up being single for a long time or even for the rest of his or her life. One must be prepared that the abundant life that Jesus came to give us may be very different from how we envision it to be. One must also refrain from offering false securities. **It is simply not true to say that God will eventually bless a Christian with a happy Christian marriage if he or she is committed to avoiding unequally yoked relationships.** This is tantamount to preaching the prosperity gospel, for Jesus offers no such promise. Jesus himself has proclaimed in Matt. 11:28-30,

"Come to me, all who labor and are heavy laden, and I will give you rest. Take my yoke upon you, and learn from me, for I am gentle and lowly in heart, and you will find rest for your souls. For my yoke is easy, and my burden is light." This is the promise that God offers. When we choose to follow his ways wholeheartedly, the ways of heaviness are lifted. We are guaranteed a life where our souls are at rest. This is joy and fulfilment on God's terms. This is peace not as the world gives but as only he alone can give (John 14:27). This is the abundant life that we must prize above the rose-tinted view of human romance as advertised by the world. Whenever we give up something for the Lord in obedience and in alignment with his ways, in the short term, it may be painful, but in the long run, we experience the joy and fulfilment that only comes about through the abundant life that Jesus gives—joy and fulfilment that only come about through the easy yoke and light burden that Jesus offers.

IMPLEMENTING AN "UNEQUALLY YOKED" STUDY SERIES IN YOUR CHURCH

A SUGGESTED PROGRAM

Churches can educate their members on this subject of unequally yoked relationships through preaching about it over the pulpit or hold specialized seminars on it. This subject can also be included as part of the Christian education program of the church, especially for the youth and young adults in the church. Included in this book is a suggested program comprising of a three-part workshop series aimed at giving participants a deeper sense of awareness concerning the key Scriptures that express God's view on unequally yoked dating and marriage relationships. The objective of this program is to help participants adopt biblical convictions about unequally yoked relationships. It is important that participants of the program be eventually convicted through Scripture rather than human wisdom that a Christian getting into a romantic relationship with a non-Christian is displeasing to God. Therefore, at the end of the program, each participant should come away with a deeper sense of awareness with regard to the key Scriptures that express God's view on unequally yoked relationships. Even though, at the end of the program, not all may be convinced and committed to not dating/marrying an unbeliever, having been exposed to the necessary Scriptures on this subject is already an extremely helpful first step in an ongoing lifelong conversation. To begin this conversation with Scripture is already the desired outcome achieved.

APPROACHING THE SUBJECT WITH SENSITIVITY

Interfaith marriage and dating is a sensitive topic because of how widespread the phenomenon is. Most Christians would know someone, either a friend or a relative who is presently entangled in interfaith dating or interfaith marriage. Due to the connections with their loved ones, teaching it as a biblical sin would no doubt be an emotional journey for church members, since, in the course of the teaching, attitudes and assumptions will be challenged. This underscores the importance of teaching subjects like these with emotional and social intelligence.

Alena Jůvová and Ondřej Duda, in their research on effective pedagogical communication, consider emotional intelligence as the ability to manage one's emotions and empathize with other people's emotions and assert that it is one of the key factors influencing the quality and effectiveness of teacher communication with students.[46] This is especially crucial when the teacher encounters students who disagree with the position being put forward by the teacher. When disagreements are verbalized, especially for sensitive topics, negative emotions from both the teacher and the students may surface. In such a scenario, applying emotional intelligence on the part of the teacher in controlling negative emotions and expressing empathy toward the students' position can lead to better pedagogical communication for the discussions ahead. The teacher can do so without necessarily endorsing the position of the students. Applying emotional intelligence in tense situations "is the ability to manage one's anger and emotions in case of conflict, with an emphasis on the need to think about the consequences. This is especially true of the teacher's ability to handle tense situations and remain calm."[47] Such timely application of emotional intelligence will produce greater confidence and trust among the participants. Other competencies related to the emotional intelligence of teachers are their active listening skills and willingness to give the participants space for self-expression. All these serve to bring about a calmer learning atmosphere which is a key criterion for quality communication.[48]

Another aspect of social and emotional intelligence is rapport building. Keith Starcher, a college teacher, conducted research on building rapport with students via one-on-one meetings that lasted about fifteen minutes each time. He made appointments with his

---

[46] Alena Jůvová and Ondřej Duda, "Emotional Intelligence Factors Helping Teachers Cope with Emotionally Tense Situations and Enhancing Effective Pedagogical Communication," *E-Pedagogium* 21, no. 2 (April 2021): 21.
[47] Jůvová and Duda, "Emotional Intelligence," 26.
[48] Jůvová and Duda, "Emotional Intelligence," 30.

students from the start of each academic year and found that it has positively impacted the rest of his time with them. In subsequent in-class surveys that he carried out with his students, he found that 95 percent of them felt more comfortable speaking out in class and asking him questions both inside and outside of the classroom. These are results that would greatly contribute to any teacher hoping to teach sensitive subjects to their cohort. Starcher concludes:

> Having completed almost 300 of these one-on-one conversations to date, I am now seeing the positive consequences of intentionally building rapport with my students. Classroom discussions flow more easily; student engagement (within and outside of the classroom) has increased; and I have more insight into the primary learning style of each student, his or her level of motivation for doing well in my class, etc. Are these one-on-one meetings worth the time? I believe they are.[49]

Rapport building is a crucial component in teaching sensitive subjects and may even achieve better results if rapport is established before the teaching sessions begin. Besides making one-on-one appointments in the course of the teaching sessions, simple gestures before the teaching session like giving each participant a private message to ask about them and how they are feeling in anticipation of the teaching could be done by teachers attempting to teach sensitive subjects. Applying such emotional and social intelligence will go a long way in establishing closer bonds with the students as the day of the teaching draws near,

---

[49] Keith Starcher, "Intentionally Building Rapport with Students," *College Teaching* 59, no. 4 (Fall 2011): 162.

paying worthwhile dividends when the teaching session finally commences.

Having clear boundaries spelled out right from the start is important in pre-empting negative emotions. As the first teaching session begins, it is worth taking time to establish some basic ground rules so that teachers and students are aware of what is deemed to be socially acceptable in the course of the project. In their article on pedagogical techniques for sensitive topics, Beth Russell, Champika Soysa, Marc Wagoner, and Lori Dawson offer a helpful list of instructions to be spelled out at the onset of the session.

> Some instructors make these environment conditions a detailed section of course syllabi, whereas others use the first course meeting to establish group standards by including students' involvement (for example, brainstorming a list of students' needs and forming a consensus on the top five class rules). Regardless of the specific practice used to establish these protections, instructors can use the following list as a launching point and a place to start the conversation, either with themselves as they construct the class or with their students on the first day: (a) everyone has a right to contribute without interruption; (b) comments should be free from insults and hurtful language and use inclusive language that invites everyone to listen; (c) non-verbal communications must be respectful as well (eye rolling, or toying with a cellphone, reading the newspaper, or focusing on other distractions while a fellow student shares an experience can be powerfully disrespectful); (d) if anyone feels slighted or offended, they should have a path of recourse through the instructor; (e) what is shared in class, stays in class; (f) share one's own experience if so inclined, but maintain the confidentiality of others (e.g., refrain from using identifying language such as 'my sister' or 'my boss'); and (g) potential or

actual physical or emotional harm to self, a minor, the elderly, or a disabled person that is current may have to be reported to relevant authorities (e.g., the Department of Social Services, depending on a given state or school policy on mandated reporting). Addressing difficult social science topics will likely be challenging for students, particularly when the course aims include prevention (and the inherent implied criticism that comes with targeting a behavior for prevention). Instructors decrease this challenge by attending to classroom environment concerns at the outset of the course.[50]

Item (f) on avoiding identifying language is particularly relevant to our context so as not to fall into the pitfall of pin-pointing actual interfaith couples in our church behind their backs. It would be awkward or worse, church relations may become strained, if the said interfaith couple got wind that their names were brought up in a discussion that specifically denounces their kind of relationship.

Another way to improve social engagement in the discussion of sensitive topics is the use of technology. Reputable web-based tools provide a trusted platform for participants to share ideas or ask questions while remaining fully anonymous. This not only provides flexibility in terms of when participants are able to find the time to key in their responses, it also offers them the luxury of time to carefully craft out what they wish to say, especially for complex ideas.[51] Having well-thought-through responses not only

---

[50] Beth S. Russell, Champika K. Soysa, Marc J. Wagoner, and Lori Dawson, "Teaching Prevention on Sensitive Topics: Key Elements and Pedagogical Techniques," *Journal of Primary Prevention* 29, no. 5 (September 1, 2008): 419.

[51] Michelle Fong, "Using Technology to Support Discussions on Sensitive Topics in the Study of Business Ethics," *Journal of Information Technology Education*, Research 14 (January 1, 2015): 249.

sharpens the participants' critical thinking abilities, it also helps them to be more sensitive and affords them the time to think twice before commenting on something controversial.[52] Such measured interaction is all the more important when it comes to sensitive topics. This would be especially helpful in collecting feedback or questions participants may have on the teaching but feel too inhibited to ask in person. Particularly for those who have a more reserved personality, the use of online tools would incentivize them to be participative in a non-threatening way.

---

[52] Fong, "Using Technology," 250.

SELECTING THE RIGHT TEACHER

It is important to select the right authority figures to be involved in the teaching of such a subject as interfaith dating/marriage. Certainly, the teacher conducting the teaching session must be someone whose marriage or dating lifestyle is not in any way contradicting the point of the teaching. Couples who are invited as guest speakers in the teaching program must also be people who not only believe in the teaching but live it out in their daily lives. For example, a Christian leader who is currently dating a non-Christian would not be suitable to teach on the subject or be a guest speaker in the teaching sessions.

Worthy role models can be an impactful force for good within the church. Israela Silberman, in his study of role models in religious settings (spiritual role modeling), observes its importance in the Jewish tradition: "Righteous people, accordingly, can serve as spiritual role models by allowing others to watch them in their everyday lives. When spiritual role models can't be observed, the same function of learning can be achieved by hearing or reading stories about their lives." [53] Silberman notes that the Talmud teaches that one could learn as much or more from the private lives of Jewish sages than their teachings, thereby affirming the huge role that spiritual role modeling plays in Jewish pedagogy. However, the reverse is also true for role models that exemplify unwholesome values or beliefs that are at odds with Scripture. In Silberman's research, he highlights spiritual role models like Osama bin Laden who became a force for evil, thus highlighting the great influence unworthy role models can also have in encouraging negative beliefs and bringing chaos to society. [54] Thus, for Christian pastoral leaders whose lives are before their congregants, it is necessary that their spiritual role modeling is well aligned with Scripture.

Clinton Parker highlights the importance of pastoral leaders in the church to be worthy role models for their congregants.

> Biblical and leadership literature stress the necessity of leadership role modeling to perpetuate desired behaviors in followers. The pastoral leader has the obligation to exemplify the very principles he or she espouses. At this point, it is important to address the fundamental distinction between a role model and a mentor. Role models are those who lead by example; they personally apply the same standard they expect their subordinates to follow. They are primarily concerned with epitomizing espoused ideals and practices for follower emulation. Personal or intimate relationships with the followers are not necessary as demonstrated by the Apostle Paul who assumed role-modeling responsibility from afar for multiple congregations in various locations

---

[53] Israela Silberman, "Spiritual Role Modeling: The Teaching of Meaning Systems, "*The International Journal for the Psychology of Religion* 13, no. 3 (2003): 177.

[54] Silberman, "Spiritual Role Modeling," 180.

including Corinth (1 Cor. 11:1), Philippi (Phil. 3:17), and Thessalonica (1 Thess. 1:6), which made closeness or intimacy unlikely.[55]

Parker proceeds to explain how mentoring is different in that mentoring requires an ongoing personal relationship to encourage, nurture, befriend, and counsel. Therefore, one need not be relationally near to be a role model, one need only be observed to be one. This means that the role of pastoral leaders is a highly influential one, since they are constantly being observed during church settings. For example, if a member of the church were to ask a pastoral leader if one is allowed to attend and celebrate the wedding of an unequally yoked marriage, what the leader does will have more influence over what he says. The leader may say that the decision on that is entirely up to the church member, yet the church member will likely take the cue from the leaders. If it is observed that the pastoral leader plans to show up for the wedding, they will do likewise. Therein lies the power of role modeling. They are watched and they will be followed.

Parker sees similarities between biblical leadership and secular organizational leadership in that both espouse the need for leaders to live out the values and behaviors that they wish to see in their followers.

> A priority of leadership is to model the way or set an example. It is inadequate for leaders to give moving speeches about vision and values. Although compelling talks offer some motivational value, followers are stimulated to action by the manner in which the leader behaves. They expect their leaders to be present, to engage,

---

[55] Clinton Parker III, "Pastoral Role Modeling as an Antecedent to Corporate Spirituality," *Journal of Religious Leadership* 13, no. 1 (Spr 2014): 169.

> and to participate in the accomplishments. It is vital that leaders capitalize on opportunities to model the values they promote. Vision and values are concrete when leaders are the examples.[56]

Parker asserts that even in secular culture, subordinates would rather follow a leader whose behavior is consistent with his or her beliefs. This brings home the point that if the message of unequally yoked relationships is to take root in the hearts of the participants, the pastoral leader teaching the subject as well as those holding key leadership positions in the church best not be involved in unequally yoked relationships. Leaders have to walk the talk.

Church members of this generation are a lot savvier when it comes to information gathering. With so much misinformation and fake news rampant in their age, they are learning how to think critically and not be overly trusting of any news source, including news from mainstream media. This is especially true for societies or countries with "low-trust" environments where fraud and criminal activity proliferate.[57] As skepticism stemming from such a climate spills over to the church context, gone are the days when church members take in whatever is said by the church leaders as authoritative. With the many scandals and stories of disgraced church leaders swirling around the internet, the people of this generation are clear that the words of leaders can only be believed if they match the way they live their lives. The prohibition of interfaith marriage and dating is a sensitive topic, and many would want to challenge such a prohibition. As it is, it is already difficult enough to find a life partner. To introduce additional limitations

---

[56] Parker, "Pastoral Role Modeling," 175.

[57] Colin Beard and John P. Wilson, *Experiential Learning: A Handbook for Education, Training and Coaching,* 3rd ed. (London: Kogan Page, 2013), 67.

to the choice of a life partner may actually cause certain individuals that could possibly be attached, to be single for life. Therefore, what we are dealing with here is a potentially divisive topic, and none will be convinced if Christian pastoral leaders do not lead by example.

By biblical standards, the ideal pedagogical framework for such education to young people are the parents:

> "Hear, O Israel: The Lord our God, the Lord is one. You shall love the Lord your God with all your heart and with all your soul and with all your might. And these words that I command you today shall be on your heart. You shall teach them diligently to your children, and shall talk of them when you sit in your house, and when you walk by the way, and when you lie down, and when you rise" (Deut. 6:4-7).

Teaching the next generation how to love the Lord wholeheartedly is the responsibility of parents. Ideally, Christian parents should be the ones instructing their children; impressing upon them the message of covenant faith every chance they have. [58] The importance of guarding one's heart and not allowing idolatrous influence to interfere with one's devotion to God and hence, the avoidance of interfaith marriage, ought to be instilled by Christian parents themselves. However, realistically speaking, not every Christian parent assumes such responsibility. Not all Christian parents see themselves as spiritual educators of their children, and even if they do, they might not feel equipped or comfortable to deal with such a topic. This is where Christian pastoral leaders come in to fill the gap, to ensure that every successive generation is exposed

---

[58] Eugene H. Merrill, *Deuteronomy,* The New American Commentary, ed. E. Ray Clendenen (Nashville: Holman Reference, 1994), 167.

to the right knowledge with regard to the Scripture's stand on interfaith marriage and dating. However, to be effective in doing so, they must be worthy role models of the anti-interfaith marriage and dating message.

PROGRAM OBJECTIVES

If the participants of the program are to be convinced by anything at all, they have to be convinced by the authority of Scripture. Therefore, the first objective is to have participants be able to single out the key Scriptures that shed light on unequally yoked relationships. These key Scriptures will serve as a reminder to them that interfaith marriage is a sin, not because of what their leaders say, but because of what God's Word says. This will not only help them to persevere in times of temptation but will also aid them in offering counsel to those who are struggling with this issue. Ultimately, it is the power of God's Word that will convict hearts and persuade minds to resist temptation and flee from unwise choices. In times of struggle, it is critical that the participants remember the Words of God rather than the instructions of men. Evaluation of this objective will be done through an open book test where they are allowed to refer to their notes or handouts. They are not required to memorize where to find the relevant Scriptures, they are only required to remember how to get to them when the need arises.

Apart from possessing the knowledge of where to find scriptural admonitions on unequally yoked relationships, participants should also be able to translate that knowledge into the understanding that Christians marrying non-Christians is unbiblical. Therefore, the second objective is to have participants consider it unbiblical to marry non-Christians. It is important that we communicate God's view on interfaith marriage clearly and scripturally to them. However, there might be some that are not immediately convinced and may need more time to digest the information or may doubt the way we interpret Scriptures. Even so, the battle is not lost, as at least the seed thought is being planted, and such participants may rethink their stand when they revisit the relevant Scriptures or when they have further interactions with other participants in the future.

FINAL THOUGHTS

I resonate with Elder John's thoughts when he says, "I have no greater joy than to hear that my children are walking in the truth" (3 John 1:4). To be able to influence the minds of fellow believers, shape their attitudes, and realign their thinking to match up with the Word of God is joy unspeakable. It is my hope that this three-part workshop program will be a satisfying and victorious experience for all who choose to conduct it. The church must do all she can to win the battle on this front, as having a godly or ungodly life partner will affect all aspects of a person's life, which would in turn affect the life of the church. There is also the need to have such a topic taught early in the life stages of God's people.

> "We encourage single Christians to make a commitment now, rather than later, to only date people who are followers of Jesus. It's much easier to make that decision when hormones aren't raging and when an attractive member of the opposite sex isn't sending off alluring vibes that he or she is interested in getting together."[59]

Offering such teachings at age groups where people are already pairing off in dating or marriage relationships might be considered late already. The ideal stage to run such a program is not after but before the age when Christian singles typically get romantically attached. This would differ depending on the country and culture. Any church seeking to teach this subject, whether it be for youth, young adults, parents, or even the whole church, could use the suggested program provided here as a guide and make adaptations where necessary. Churches may customize the program to fit their cultures, but one needs to be sure that the teachings of Scripture must remain as the unshakable bedrock to the program. This

---

[59] Strobel and Strobel, *Spiritual Mismatch*, 190.

program works because every exhortation stems from the Word. Any shift in attitudes or new conviction forged must be persuaded through the Word. The role of the teacher is to teach the Word and facilitate the discussion around the Word. This must be the non-negotiable foundation to this unequally yoked teaching.

One key recommendation that I would like to propose is for churches to consider preaching a sermon on unequally yoked relationships to "prepare the ground" first before embarking on the program. As this is a sensitive topic, it might be a good idea to make sure that the whole church is on board; that the whole church knows what God's Word says about this topic before starting on a specialized program on the subject. I preached such a sermon some years back when I was preaching through the book of Malachi in my church. It was immensely helpful to have my entire church be on the same page with regards to unequally yoked romantic relationships. The full script of my sermon can be found in the next chapter.

PREACHING IT

Title: **God's Expectations of Us (Part 4)**

Scripture: **Malachi 2:10-12** *(ESV)*

Today's passage deals with the topic of interfaith marriages. To be clear, I am talking about interfaith marriages and not interracial marriages. So, let's get that distinction cleared up. The Bible has got nothing against interracial marriages. Interfaith marriages are marriages where each partner comes from a different religion. For the purpose of today's sermon, when we talk about interfaith marriage, we are specifically referring to God's people; God's covenant community, marrying people that are outside of the covenant community.

This issue of interfaith marriage was a huge problem back in Malachi's days and is also a huge problem for us today in New Testament times. The issue of Christians, God's people, God's covenant community, getting into a romantic relationship with non-Christians is still a big struggle for many singles today. But let us not forget that today's Malachi passage is set within the framework of God's unmerited love for His people. We see that right from the start of Malachi in chapter 1 verse 2. "I have loved you," says the Lord." So, we need to bear in mind that God is saying all these because He loves His people and dearly want what is best for them. With that in mind, let's take a deep dive into this topic as we see how God's word can shed light on this subject of interfaith marriage.

Malachi 2:10-12 says: **¹⁰Do we not all have one Father? Did not one God create us? Why do we profane the covenant of our ancestors by being unfaithful to one another? ¹¹Judah has been unfaithful. A detestable thing has been committed in Israel and**

in Jerusalem: Judah has desecrated the sanctuary the Lord loves by marrying women who worship a foreign god. [12]As for the man who does this, whoever he may be, may the Lord remove him from the tents of Jacob—even though he brings an offering to the Lord Almighty.

Today's passage is centred upon this theme of interfaith marriages where God's people inter-marry with people who are not God's people. And such interfaith marriages; the act of marrying a person who worships a foreign god is considered to be a detestable act to God. So why are interfaith marriages so detestable to God? Well, the passage begins with one God, and this one God is our Father whom we are attached to or bonded to, by kinship. So, this passage begins with a picture of a holy family consisting of God and His covenant people. However, when God's people inter-marry with pagans who are still worshipping their pagan gods, something foreign, something ungodly, something idolatrous is being introduced into this holy family and God calls this a desecration of His beloved sanctuary. In other words, God's holy space is being invaded by foreign elements. To introduce a foreign element into this holy family by means of an interfaith marriage, verse 10 makes clear that such an act is also a breach of faith to one another. Meaning, when a person is involved in an interfaith marriage, that person not only lets God down, he or she lets the entire community down as well. Interfaith marriage is a major violation to our bond with this one God, and our bond with God's covenant community and God called out interfaith marriages to be a detestable act and an act of unfaithfulness. In fact, in verse 12, God says that a person who commits such a detestable act should be excommunicated; put out of fellowship even if he is very generous and make great contributions and donations to God's work. To act generously and piously in God's holy sanctuary while at the same time desecrating His holy sanctuary is simply inconsistent, so God is saying, "who cares about his contributions, kick him out of my sanctuary!" The severity of the punishment reveals to us the severity of this sin of interfaith marriages.

God forbidding interfaith marriages has always been consistently spelled out throughout the Old Testament Scriptures. What we have up on the slide is a list of some of these Scriptures. Exodus 34:16; Deuteronomy 7:3-4; 1 Kings 11:1-9; 16:31; Ezra 9 & 10; Nehemiah 10:30, 13:23-31. But because of time, let's examine just one of them in the list.

Deuteronomy 7:3-4 says: **³Do not intermarry with them. Do not give your daughters to their sons or take their daughters for your sons, ⁴for they will turn your children away from following me to serve other gods, and the Lord's anger will burn against you and will quickly destroy you.**

These are God's specific instructions for Israel to prohibit them from interfaith marriages after their conquest of Canaan. The reason given is that interfaith marriages **will**–the Bible did not say maybe, the Bible says **will** cause God's people to fall away towards idolatry. God, in His infinite wisdom, highlights the fact that interfaith marriages **will** always cause His people to fall away and not the other way round. There has never ever been any sort of suggestion in the Scriptures for God's people to get married to pagan spouses in order to bring their pagan spouses into the faith– never ever. Now in the New Testament, there are suggestions as to what you can do to influence your spouse if one party happened to convert to Christianity while already being in a marriage. But this is a situation where two non-Christians are already in a marriage and then one party suddenly converts; this is a vastly different situation from an unmarried Christian, wanting to convert their future spouse through marriage. Totally different situation. In other words, using marriage as mission work is not biblical. There is zero support in the Bible for so-called "missionary marriages." Even the wisest of all human kings, King Solomon himself was drawn into idolatry through interfaith marriages. Well, some people may think that they are better than Solomon; that perhaps they can keep following Jesus after being married to an unbelieving spouse, and that they are trusting in God's grace to see them through. Somebody once ask: "If I were to marry a non-Christian, will God's grace be there to see me through?" That is like asking: "If I were to intentionally chop off my arm, will God's grace be there to see me through?" Of course, God's grace will be there; our Father's love and grace will always be there to carry us through despite our disobedience. But isn't it so much better to live life with both arms intact? Why would we want to disobey God and grieve the Father's heart by presuming upon His grace? Our responsibility as Christians is not to presume upon God's grace and act on the possibility of what God may do, but to act on what God has already told us, in His word. In other words, we do what God have instructed us to do rather than disobeying His instructions by presuming upon His grace.

Marriage is meant to be a beautiful act of worship and service unto the Lord. But when we intentionally go against God's instructions on marriage and choose to put our own needs above God's rule over our lives, this act of worship becomes an act of idolatry which explains why God would use such strong language against it in Malachi 2:11.

Now let's move on to the New Testament. A couple of verses there offers the implication that the Old Testament prohibition on interfaith marriages still stands. The most famous one being the unequally yoked passage found in 2 Corinthians 6:14.

2 Corinthians 6:14 says: **[14]Do not be yoked together with unbelievers. For what do righteousness and wickedness have in common? Or what fellowship can light have with darkness?**

Admittedly, the context of this passage is not talking about interfaith marriages, so what is Paul talking about here? The verse before this says: **[13]As a fair exchange—I speak as to my children—open wide your hearts also.** If you launch out on a study of this passage, you will find that Paul here, is pleading with the Corinthians to open their hearts to him because he is trying to convince them that he is a true apostle of Jesus Christ. So, on the one hand, Paul urges them to open their hearts to him, and on the other hand, he is also pleading with the Corinthians not to open their hearts to false teachers who are leading them towards idolatry. Therefore, it is in such a false teacher and idolatry context that Paul says do not be unequally yoked with them. So admittedly, the context here is not about marriages yet it is very appropriate to apply this unequally yoked principle to the marriage context. This is because essentially, the unequally yoked principle is saying: whoever you open your heart to, you will be like that person. That person whom you open your heart to, will shape your values and beliefs. Just like two oxen being yoked together, or joined together working the field, you will walk in the way in which that person is walking because they will be very influential in steering the direction of your life. It is no wonder then that Paul persuades the Corinthians to open their hearts to himself and not to the false teachers. In other words, whoever you open your heart to, that person will greatly influence your faith and practice. Therefore, this unequally yoked principle can be applied to all sorts of relationships and it is especially relevant to the marriage relationship. So just because the text is not specifically addressing the context of marriage doesn't mean you can't take the unequally yoked principle and apply it to other contexts like marriage or business partnerships. Yet, as always, if we do have a New Testament text that specifically addresses the marriage context, all the better! And for such a New Testament text, we go to 1 Corinthians 7:39.

1 Corinthians 7:39 says: **[39]A woman is bound to her husband as long as he lives. But if her husband dies, she is free to marry anyone she wishes, but he must belong to the Lord.**

Here is a New Testament text that is specifically addressing the context of marriage. Paul is giving instructions to widows, telling them that if they were to remarry, they must make sure that the new spouse belongs to the Lord; that the new spouse must be a Christian. So, this is a clear and direct verse that gives us the confidence to believe that the Old Testament prohibition on interfaith marriages still stands till today. In contrast, you will not find a single verse in the New Testament that even remotely suggest that the interfaith marriage prohibition had been lifted. Therefore, to disregard this prohibition today is to disobey Scripture and therefore interfaith marriage in today's context should rightly be understood as a sin. So, let's be clear that the biblical theology of interfaith marriages points to it being a sin; from Old Testament to New Testament, it is a sin. It is disobedience to Scripture.

With that in mind, let us now ask the big question: what does God expect of us today? How should such a theology express itself practically in the church? First and foremost, our instruction to all our young people or to Christian singles in our midst must be very clear and precise: interfaith marriage is a sin, it is disobedience to Scripture. Now, when you give a clear-cut instruction like that, especially to a group of young people, usually, you'll get a counter-question. And this counter-question tends to sound something like this: "Can I go ahead and date non-Christians but if they fail to convert to Christianity, then I will be sure to pull the handbrakes and call it quits because I will make the resolve not to marry an unbeliever no matter what! How about that?"

Let us firstly define dating as being in a romantic relationship for the consideration of moving towards marriage. With that definition in mind, my first question to the Christian would be: "Are you being fair to the non-Christian?" You go dating with a non-Christian, captured his heart, and just because he won't convert, you call it quits, leaving him to nurse a broken heart. Is that a loving thing to do? Is that Christ-like behavior? Well, you might say: "It is fair as long as he knows my stand right from the start and he agrees to such an arrangement, so when all the relevant information is out there, the guy is entering into the arrangement with eyes wide open, then all is fair!"

Then my next question is: "Are you sure you can apply the handbrakes and pull out of the relationship when it is time to do so?" I came across an article before about romantic relationships being likened to rearing tiger cubs in your home. Baby tigers are deceptively cute and cuddly, so once you bring them into your home, you think you are the owner and you think you are able to contain their ferocity. The fact is, you may be the owner of a tiger but you are by no means its master. Before you know it, the tiger will grow so huge and strong that it will pounce on you and overpower you. So it is with romantic relationships, they tend to have a life of their own after some time and before you know it, you find yourself overpowered by it. So young people and singles out there, please don't go keeping a tiger as a pet in your home.

John Piper, in a podcast interview, calls dating a non-Christian a sin. He says that dating a non-Christian puts you on a trajectory towards disobeying 1 Corinthains 7:39 which is the verse we examined earlier on. John Piper says: "First Corinthians 7:39 says that we are to marry "only in the Lord." And if you are on a trajectory to fall in love with and marry a woman who is outside the Lord, you are on a trajectory to disobey this text. And to be on a trajectory to disobey a text is to disobey a text."

So Christian parents, if your child is on a trajectory to disobey 1 Corinthians 7:39; if your child wish to date a non-Christian, do not give him or her your blessing. Tell them that mummy and daddy disapprove because the end goal of dating is marriage and getting into interfaith marriages is disobedience to Scripture.

My wife and I have been doing pre-marital counseling for years. It is a very meaningful ministry because healthy churches consist of healthy families and pre-marital counseling helps couples be off to a healthy start. But if you think about it, by the time couples sign up for pre-marital counseling, it is a little bit late already because usually, by that time, the wedding date is already set, the restaurant is already booked, the deposits have all been paid up. What if in the midst of the pre-marital counseling, we find that one of them is really not a believer? Then what do you expect us to do? Tell them to call off the wedding and forgo their deposits? So, the time to communicate such a message is really when they are in their youth, when they have yet to enter into dating relationships, because once young people start dating, it is already too late. So, parents, you need to have this talk with your youth and you must do it before, not after.

In a 2013 interview with Christianity Today, Dr Russell Moore, who was then, the president of the Southern Baptist Convention's Ethics and Religious Liberty Commission, this is what he has to say about the issue of interfaith marriages. Dr Russell Moore says: "We live in the world as it is, and we love our unbelieving neighbors. Christians are going to be drawn toward some of those unbelievers and wish to join themselves to them in marriage. That's where the church should graciously speak the hard word that marriage isn't just about romance, but also about gospel and mission. Some will hear this and go away angry or saddened. But some will hear in these hard words the voice they heard at the very beginning of their call to Christ: "Take up your cross and follow me.""

For our young people to make that difficult choice to impose biblical restrictions upon their choice of a life partner, that is going to take sacrifice, it is not going to be easy. Dr Russell Moore sees this difficult path as part and parcel of taking up our cross and following Jesus. So, parents, this is how we should frame it–it is part of discipleship; part of being a follower of Jesus.

Then the next question is: "How then, do we know if that somebody is a Christian or not?" This is tricky because just because a person goes to church does not mean he or she is a Christian. Even a person who is baptized doesn't mean he or she is a Christian. There are countless examples of people who got baptized, and then got married, and then suddenly, you don't see them in church anymore. So, we really need to observe a person's life testimony and be very discerning–who is a Christian and who is not. So, do not be deceived, anybody can claim to be a Christian, but is this person truly living for Jesus? We need to take this evaluation very seriously because it is clear from the Scriptures that God does not take this sin of interfaith marriage lightly.

Now, how about interfaith dating couples who are not married yet, but are currently in a romantic dating relationship, what then is the right thing to do? I believe the word for this situation is repentance. What is repentance? Repentance in the Greek is metanoia – which means "change of mind." You once thought that it is fine to date and marry an unbeliever, but now, you metanoia–you change your mind and you now believe and confess that it is not okay. You now recognise that it is a sin; you have changed your mind about it. This change of mind should lead you to make a U-turn on your interfaith dating relationship. This is not going to be easy, but yes, break off from your romantic dating relationship and help your non-Christian friend know that the most important relationship he should be focussing on right now, is his relationship with God. So, rest assured that it is never too late to repent; to metanoia and get back on track with God's Word and God's ways.

So, if you are somehow entangled in an unequally yoked relationship right now, the last thing I want for you is to feel condemned. Far from feeling condemned, we should feel loved. Yes, feel loved by God. I know it's kind of counter intuitive, but really, instead of feeling condemned, we should feel loved because God our Father loves us enough to set such boundaries for us. We may not fully understand the wisdom of God in this but we trust that all boundaries that God set for us, is for our own good because He loves us so much, He wants us to be blessed in every area of our lives. God is for our flourishment!

The next question on our mind then is–what if the interfaith marriage sin is already committed? The couple has knowingly entered into such a sin, how do we, as a church move on from there? This is a very deep question that involves complex analysis of Old Testament and New Testament Scriptures but we shall not go there today because my time is almost up. To keep it short and simple, as a church, we must not have this holier than thou attitude and think of such couples as second class because they may have stumbled in this area, but hey, we are also sinful in other areas; we are no better, we too are sinners in our own way. Bottom line is– the church is a place of acceptance and healing for those who are hurting and so we do need to exercise love and compassion to all such couples.

Let me now end with these words of wisdom from Proverbs 31. Verse 30 says: **[30]Charm is deceptive, and beauty is fleeting; but a woman who fears the Lord is to be praised.**

Allow me to offer a parting question to all the singles out there. What would most attract you to your potential spouse? The most precious and important quality for a potential spouse; the number one thing that you should be looking for, is fear of the Lord. Yet this is the one thing that you can never find in a non-Christian. So, to all the singles out there, we need to get our priorities right. And to the rest of us in this church family, we really need to pray for our young people, because they are facing so many temptations in this area. So let us close this time, by praying for them.

Dear Father God,

We pray for all the young people in our church.

We pray that You will help them to make wise choices.

*Help them to detest what is detestable to You
and esteem what You esteem.*

We ask all these in Jesus' name, Amen.

A SUGGESTED PROGRAM

SUGGESTED PROGRAM OUTLINE

**A Christian's Guide to Dating and Marriage:
A Series of Three Workshop Sessions**

Session One:

- ❖ **Worship**
- ❖ **Icebreakers**
- ❖ **Lesson** (Purpose of dating)
- ❖ **Break**
- ❖ **Lesson** (Honesty in dating)
- ❖ **Group Discussion** (Important non-negotiables)
- ❖ **Q&A**

Session Two:

- ❖ **Worship**
- ❖ **Recap**
- ❖ **Lesson** (OT texts on interfaith marriages: part 1)
- ❖ **Group Discussion** (King Solomon and King Ahab)
- ❖ **Break**
- ❖ **Lesson** (OT texts on interfaith marriages: part 2)
- ❖ **Q&A**

Session Three:

- ❖ **Worship**
- ❖ **Recap**
- ❖ **Lesson** (NT texts on interfaith marriages)
- ❖ **Break**
- ❖ **Group Discussion** (4 questions)
- ❖ **Q&A**

Possible addition to the program: Guest Couple Interview

SESSION ONE WORKSHEET

Part 1: Purpose of Dating

1) Why do we date?

2) How do I ascertain if I can envision a person being my life partner or not?

3) How can I find out more about the person besides actually dating the person?

The Point:

There is an objective endpoint to dating:
checking each other out to see if we want
to make a lifelong commitment to each other.
Dating should always be done with marriage in mind.

When checking each other out (dating), we may not be totally honest with each other. Daters may pretend to be someone he/she is not.

> E.g. pretend to enjoy action movies to please the other party so as not to risk being rejected. Movie tastes are not such a serious matter, but what if more serious matters like personal values are in conflict? E.g. your dater is not committed to attending church regularly. Yet because you like the person so much, you pretend that it is not a big deal.

> E.g. you observe that your dater is very boastful and is always bragging, and you do not like it. Yet you pretend that you are not the least bit bothered by it as you find it difficult to talk to your dater about it honestly.

4) What is holding people back from being honest?

5) Do you think it is important to confront conflicting values with your dater honestly? Why?

6) What if my dater refuses to change after I confront him/her with a very
   important matter that I deeply value?

Group Discussion

List all the things that are important to you that you would want your
dater/life partner to live up to. Appoint a leader to present your list after
fifteen minutes.

The Point:

Understand what are the non-negotiables
that are so important to you in a life partner that
you will commit to not compromise on them no matter what.

SESSION TWO WORKSHEET

Recap:

- ❖ As Christians, we consider dating as being in a romantic relationship for the consideration of moving toward marriage. Therefore, we are checking out the suitability of the dater before we make a lifelong commitment to the person. Thus, dating for the Christian is purposeful and goal specific.

- ❖ Because of this goal-specific purpose, dating is a good time to be honest with each other and confront conflicting values early. We all have our negotiable and non-negotiable values, and if significant conflicting values cannot be resolved, we either break up the dating relationship or go for counseling. There is no shame in either.

Part 1: OT Texts on Interfaith Marriages (Moses's Law, King Solomon and King Ahab)

A) Understanding the term 'interfaith marriage."

God's covenant community marrying outside of the covenant community.

B) The interfaith marriage prohibition as spelled out in the Law of Moses.

Exodus 34:11-17 (ESV)

[11] "Observe what I command you this day. Behold, I will drive out before you the Amorites, the Canaanites, the Hittites, the Perizzites, the Hivites, and the Jebusites. [12] Take care, lest you make a covenant with the inhabitants of the land to which you go, lest it become a snare in your midst. [13] You shall tear down their altars and break their pillars and cut down their Asherim [14] (for you shall worship no other god, for the Lord, whose name is Jealous, is a jealous God), [15] lest you make a covenant with the inhabitants of the land, and when they whore after their gods and sacrifice to their gods and you are invited, you eat of his sacrifice, [16] and **you take of their daughters for your sons,** and their daughters whore after their gods and make your sons whore after their gods. [17] "You shall not make for yourself any gods of cast metal.

Deuteronomy 7:3-4 (NIV)

³ **Do not intermarry with them.** Do not give your daughters to their sons or take their daughters for your sons, ⁴ for **they will turn your children away** from following me to serve other gods, and the Lord's anger will burn against you and will quickly destroy you.

1) **As can be seen in Exodus 34:16, what is God's concern in allowing interfaith marriage?**

2) **Read Deuteronomy 7:3-4. List down the chain of events that will eventually lead to God's people being destroyed.**

Group Discussion

CASE STUDY 1: King Solomon's interfaith marriages

1 Kings 11:1-9 (ESV)

¹ Now King Solomon loved many foreign women, along with the daughter of Pharaoh: Moabite, Ammonite, Edomite, Sidonian, and Hittite women, ² from the nations concerning which the Lord had said to the people of Israel, "You shall not enter into marriage with them, neither shall they with you, for surely they will turn away your heart after their gods." Solomon clung to these in love. ³ He had 700 wives, who were princesses, and 300 concubines. And his wives turned away his heart. ⁴ For when Solomon was old his wives turned away his heart after other gods, and his heart was not wholly true to the Lord his God, as was the heart of David his father. ⁵ For Solomon went after Ashtoreth the goddess of the Sidonians, and after Milcom the abomination of the Ammonites. ⁶ So Solomon did what was evil in the sight of the Lord and did not wholly follow the Lord, as David his father had done. ⁷ Then Solomon built a high place for Chemosh the abomination of Moab, and for Molech the abomination of the Ammonites, on the mountain east of Jerusalem. ⁸ And so he did for all his foreign wives, who made offerings and sacrificed to their gods. ⁹ And the Lord was angry with Solomon, because his heart

had turned away from the Lord, the God of Israel, who had appeared to him twice.

1) What were God's instructions on marriage (v. 2)? Why?

2) What caused Solomon's heart to be turned away from God?

3) What did Solomon end up doing (v. 6)?

4) How did God feel about all this?

5) What if an Israelite, during Solomon's time, felt that his faith is strong enough to disobey God's instructions and marry "foreign women" and still not turn away from God? How would you advise such a person?

CASE STUDY 2: King Ahab's interfaith marriage with Jezebel

1 Kings 16:25-33 (ESV)

[25] Omri did what was evil in the sight of the Lord, and did more evil than all who were before him. [26] For he walked in all the way of Jeroboam the son of Nebat, and in the sins that he made Israel to sin, provoking the Lord, the God of Israel, to anger by their idols. [27] Now the rest of the acts of Omri that he did, and the might that he showed, are they not written in the Book of the Chronicles of the Kings of Israel? [28] And Omri slept with his fathers and was buried in Samaria, and Ahab his son reigned in his place. [29] In the thirty-eighth year of Asa king of Judah, Ahab the son of Omri began to reign over Israel, and Ahab the son of Omri reigned over Israel in Samaria twenty-two years. [30] And Ahab the son of Omri did evil in the sight of the Lord, more than all who were before him. [31] And as if it had been a light thing for him to walk in the sins of Jeroboam the son of Nebat, he took for his wife Jezebel the daughter of Ethbaal king of the Sidonians, and went and served Baal and worshiped him. [32] He erected an altar for Baal in the house of Baal, which he built in Samaria. [33] And Ahab made an Asherah. Ahab did more to provoke the Lord, the God of Israel, to anger than all the kings of Israel who were before him.

Background: Jeroboam is the first king that led the newly divided kingdom of Israel into idolatry with two golden calves (one in Bethel and one in Dan) – 1 Kings 12:25-33.

1) Read v. 26. Omri followed Jeroboam's example in sinning. What sin is that?

2) Read v. 31. Omri's son, Ahab, also followed Jeroboam's example in sinning, but added to that grave sin is another grave sin. What is that?

3) What did Jezebel introduce to Ahab and Israel?

4) How did that make God feel?

Ezra 10:2-3 (ESV)

[2] And Shecaniah the son of Jehiel, of the sons of Elam, addressed Ezra: "We have **broken faith** with our God and have **married foreign women** from the peoples of the land, but even now there is hope for Israel in spite of this. [3] Therefore let us make a covenant with our God to put away all these wives and their children, according to the counsel of my lord and of those who tremble at the commandment of our God, and let it be done according to the Law.

1) How did the people "broke faith?" (v. 2)

Nehemiah 13:23-31 (ESV)

[23] In those days also I saw the Jews who had married women of Ashdod, Ammon, and Moab. [24] And half of their children spoke the language of Ashdod, and they could not speak the language of Judah, but only the language of each people. [25] And I confronted them and cursed them and beat some of them and pulled out their hair. And I made them take an oath in the name of God, saying, "You shall not give your daughters to their sons, or take their daughters for your sons or for yourselves. [26] Did not Solomon king of Israel sin on account of such women? Among the many nations there was no king like him, and he was beloved by his God, and God made him king over all Israel. Nevertheless, foreign women made even him to sin. [27] Shall we then listen to you and do all this great evil and act treacherously against our God by marrying foreign women?" [28] And one of the sons of Jehoiada, the son of Eliashib the high priest, was the son-in-law of Sanballat the Horonite. Therefore I chased him from me. [29] Remember them, O my God, because they have desecrated the priesthood and the covenant of the priesthood and the Levites. [30] Thus I cleansed them from everything foreign, and I established the duties of the priests and Levites, each in his work; [31] and I provided for the wood offering at appointed times, and for the firstfruits.

2) What was it that Nehemiah found to be so detestable? Why?

SESSION THREE WORKSHEET

Recap:

- ❖ Previously, we started off by looking at Exodus 34 and Deuteronomy 7, which show us that this prohibition against interfaith marriage is part of Moses's Law and its strong connection with idolatry.

- ❖ Then we looked at how King Solomon, as well as King Ahab, were led astray to idolatry through interfaith marriages, and in so doing, provoked God to anger.

- ❖ Then we looked into Ezra and Nehemiah and again saw a consistent message against interfaith marriages.

NT Texts on Interfaith Marriages

2 Corinthians 6:13-14 (ESV)

[13]In return (I speak as to children) widen your hearts also.

[14]Do not be unequally yoked with unbelievers. For what partnership has righteousness with lawlessness? Or what fellowship has light with darkness?

1) What do you think Paul is talking about in v. 13?

2) Since the context surrounding this unequally yoked passage is not specifically addressing marriages, is it still appropriate to apply this unequally yoked principle to the marriage context?

3) Is there an interfaith marriage prohibition verse in the New Testament that is specifically written in the marriage context?

1 Corinthians 7:39 (NIV)

[39] A woman is bound to her husband as long as he lives. But if her husband dies, she is free to marry anyone she wishes, but he must belong to the Lord.

4) How would you interpret such a verse?

Ephesians 5:22-32 (ESV)

[22] Wives, submit to your own husbands, as to the Lord. [23] For the husband is the head of the wife even as Christ is the head of the church, his body, and is himself its Savior. [24] Now as the church submits to Christ, so also wives should submit in everything to their husbands. [25] Husbands, love your wives, as Christ loved the church and gave himself up for her, [26] that he might sanctify her, having cleansed her by the washing of water with the word, [27] so that he might present the church to himself in splendor, without spot or wrinkle or any such thing, that she might be holy and without blemish. [28] In the same way husbands should love their wives as their own bodies. He who loves his wife loves himself. [29] For no one ever hated his own flesh, but nourishes and cherishes it, just as Christ does the church, [30] because we are members of his body. [31] "Therefore a man shall leave his father and mother and hold fast to his wife, and the two shall become one flesh." [32] This mystery is profound, and I am saying that it refers to Christ and the church.

5) For the Christian, what is marriage meant to reflect?

6) Can an interfaith marriage reflect this God-given picture of marriage?

The Point:

For those who demand NT evidence
that the interfaith marriage prohibition still stands,
you can offer them these passages, particularly 1 Corinthians 7:39.
At the same time, be mindful that there is not a single verse in the NT
that even remotely suggests that the prohibition has been lifted.
So, it is clear that the prohibition is there in the OT and also in the NT.
Therefore, to enter into an unequally yoked relationship
is to disobey Scripture and that is a sin.

1) Share one practical way to avoid getting into an unequally yoked relationship.

2) List all the practical problems you can think of which may arise when a Christian gets into an unequally yoked marriage relationship.

3) How should we advise Christians who feel tempted to get into an unequally yoked relationship?

4) How should we treat Christians who are already attached or married to an unbeliever?

The Point:

This unequally yoked issue does have a tendency
to drive Christians away from the church,
so our number one thought should be how to help the unequally yoked
stay in the church–how to help them feel accepted,
even in the midst of their sin.
This is tough because people tend to feel judged
when they are in such a sin and attending church at the same time.

GUEST COUPLE INTERVIEW

A possible addition to your program lineup is to invite a Christian couple from your church for an interview with them. This is to allow their testimony to inspire the participants to trust in God for their love life. Give the guest couple the interview questions in advance so they can pray about it and prepare their answers in advance. Here are some suggested guest couple interview questions:

1) **How did it all begin between the two of you?**

2) **Throughout your romance journey, were both of you open to dating or marrying a non-Christian? Why?**

3) **Were both of you intentionally looking for someone with some criteria in mind? If yes, what were they?**

4) **How were both of you trusting God for a life partner when you were still single?**

5) **Any final advice to all the singles here?**

OPEN BOOK TEST

Q1) Your schoolmate refuses to believe that the Law of Moses prohibits interfaith marriage. List two places in Scripture that you can point out to this schoolmate of yours.

Q2) Which chapter in 1 Kings records God's anger with King Solomon's interfaith marriages?

Q3) Which chapter in 1 Kings records God's anger with King Ahab for his interfaith marriage with Jezebel?

Q4) Where in the book of Ezra do we see interfaith marriage being understood as unfaithfulness?

Q5) Which chapter in the book of Nehemiah do we see Nehemiah being so mad at the people's interfaith marriages?

Q6) Your non-Christian friend just came across the term "unequally yoked" and ask you if that term is even found in the Bible. Where can you direct her to find it in the Bible?

Q7) That same non-Christian friend kept insisting that using the "unequally yoked' principle on marriage is to use it out of context. What other verse in the New Testament can you direct her to?

TEACHER'S GUIDE

SESSION ONE

Part 1: Purpose of Dating

1) Why do we date?

So that we can discover the suitability of our potential life partner–to work toward marriage.

- ❖ *Dating is not for casual fun or a cure for loneliness.*
- ❖ *Do not date somebody whom you cannot envision being married to for life. We need to be loving and not contribute to the hurt of others. People do feel rejected when the dating ends.*

2) How do I ascertain if I can envision a person being my life partner or not?

There is usually a spectrum: on one end, we have "very sure not my type," and on the other end is "very infatuated with this person." So, we need to find out more about the person if we do have a slight interest in that person. The key question to ask is:

3) How can I find out more about the person besides actually dating the person?

Social media, observe from afar, go out in groups. (Consider dating to find out even more about the person as people can be different in a one-to-one context as compared to a group setting.)

The Point:

There is an objective endpoint to dating:
checking each other out to see if we want
to make a lifelong commitment to each other.
Dating should always be done with marriage in mind.

Part 2: Honesty in Dating

When checking each other out (dating), we may not be totally honest with each other. Daters may pretend to be someone he/she is not.

E.g. pretend to enjoy action movies to please the other party so as not to risk being rejected. Movie tastes are not such a serious matter, but what if more serious matters like personal values are in conflict? E.g. your dater is not committed to attending church regularly. Yet because you like the person so much, you pretend that it is not a big deal.

E.g. you observe that your dater is very boastful and is always bragging, and you do not like it. Yet you pretend that you are not the least bit bothered by it as you find it difficult to talk to your dater about it honestly.

4) What is holding people back from being honest?

Fear of rejection/insecurity–because we are not secure in Jesus. In other words, we are desperate–desperate for the relationship to work out. It is normal to feel a bit desperate, especially when you have been single for a long time. However, we do not want to be overly desperate, or else we will be short-changing ourselves and making an idol out of our dater.

Sometimes, people think that they can just wait it out in the dating phase and simply change their partners when they get married, but that is usually wishful thinking. If a person cannot change during dating, usually it is even harder to get the person to change after marriage. Dating is the time to confront conflicting values.

5) Do you think it is important to confront conflicting values with your dater honestly? Why?

We need to confront conflicting values early when we are not so invested in the relationship, so we know if the dater is open to change or not.

> *E.g. someone who is not a saver and is irresponsible with finances, if we refuse to deal with it during dating, we can expect the same in marriage.*

"Do not rebuke a mocker or he will hate you; rebuke a wise man and he will love you" (Prov. 9:8). One of the most important things you can figure out in dating is how the person responds to you when you bring up problematic issues for discussion. A wise person is grateful for information that will help the relationship or help him/her to be a better person. A mocker will get angry and defensive when confronted. In other words, how your dater responds to confrontation helps you diagnose what kind of person he/she is.

When we are so infatuated with someone, we tend to lose touch with our values.

> *E.g. we value mutual respect. But when we are "in love," sometimes we allow the person to speak to us disrespectfully. Over time, if we fail to confront the dater, such behaviors start to normalize. So the key is to be in touch with our values right from the start and be upfront with the person early in the dating relationship because our values matter. What we*

tolerate is what we will get. We must make our values the standard that our dater must live up to.

Take an early stand on what is important to you. We should not settle, but at the same time, we should also be realistic. Nobody is perfect, we are all sinners.

E.g. if your standard is that your dater must attend prayer meetings every week, some Christians may not be able to live up to that.

We must take responsibility for being upfront with our values. The onus is on you to express yourself during dating. If you choose to suffer in silence just to stay in the dating relationship rather than having a healthy discussion with your dater, then the fault is on you for not being honest in the relationship.

6) What if my dater refuses to change after I confront him/her with a very important matter that I deeply value?

Then this means you either break up the dating relationship or you both go for counseling with a mature Christian couple. There is no shame in either. Remember that the objective of dating is NOT marriage. The objective of dating is to assess the suitability of a potential life partner and therefore, breaking up is by no means considered a failure, but success. You have succeeded in uncovering the suitability of your dater. The dating objective has been met with success.

Group Discussion

List all the things that are important to you that you would want your dater/life partner to live up to. Appoint a leader to present your list after fifteen minutes.

Some Examples: Humorous, Respectful, Honest, Loyal, Caring, Humble, Love animals, Not hot-tempered, Considerate, Not a smoker, Gentle, Mature, Communicative, Empathetic, Good listener, Diligent, Does not speak vulgarities, Kind, Churchgoing Christian.

The Point:
**Understand what are the non-negotiables
that are so important to you in a life partner that
you will commit to not compromise on them no matter what.**

SESSION TWO

Recap:

- ❖ As Christians, we consider dating as being in a romantic relationship for the consideration of moving toward marriage. Therefore, we are checking out the suitability of the dater before we make a lifelong commitment to the person. Thus, dating for the Christian is purposeful and goal specific.

- ❖ Because of this goal-specific purpose, dating is a good time to be honest with each other and confront conflicting values early. We all have our negotiable and non-negotiable values, and if significant conflicting values cannot be resolved, we either break up the dating relationship or go for counseling. There is no shame in either.

Part 1: OT Texts on Interfaith Marriages (Moses's Law, King Solomon and King Ahab)

A) Understanding the term 'interfaith marriage."

When you read commentaries on this topic, some will use the term inter-marriage. Some will use the term mixed marriages, and they all refer to the same thing, which is God's people marrying people of other faiths. But these terms in modern usage can also refer to interracial marriages, so to avoid confusion, I use the term interfaith marriage. However, that can also refer to, for example, a Muslim marrying a Hindu. So, in our context, we are specifically referring to God's covenant community marrying outside of the covenant community.

B) The interfaith marriage prohibition as spelled out in the Law of Moses.

Exodus 34:11-17 (ESV)

[11] "Observe what I command you this day. Behold, I will drive out before you the Amorites, the Canaanites, the Hittites, the Perizzites, the Hivites, and the Jebusites. [12] Take care, lest you make a covenant with the inhabitants of the land to which you go, lest it become a snare in your midst. [13] You shall tear down their altars and break their pillars and cut down their Asherim [14] (for you shall worship no other god, for the Lord, whose name is Jealous, is a jealous God), [15] lest you make a covenant with the inhabitants of the land, and when they whore after their gods and sacrifice to their gods and you are invited, you eat of his sacrifice, [16] and **you take of their daughters for your sons**, and their daughters whore after their gods and make your sons whore after their gods. [17] "You shall not make for yourself any gods of cast metal.

Deuteronomy 7:3-4 (NIV)

[3] **Do not intermarry with them.** Do not give your daughters to their sons or take their daughters for your sons, [4] for **they will turn your children away** from following me to serve other gods, and the Lord's anger will burn against you and will quickly destroy you.

1) **As can be seen in Exodus 34:16, what is God's concern in allowing interfaith marriage?**

People of other faiths leading God's people towards idolatry

2) **Read Deuteronomy 7:3-4. List down the chain of events that will eventually lead to God's people being destroyed.**

Interfaith marriage > God's people being influenced towards idolatry > arousal of God's anger > destruction of God's people.

Group Discussion

CASE STUDY 1: King Solomon's interfaith marriages

1 Kings 11:1-9 (ESV)

[1] Now King Solomon loved many foreign women, along with the daughter of Pharaoh: Moabite, Ammonite, Edomite, Sidonian, and Hittite women, [2] from the nations concerning which the Lord had said to the people of Israel, "You shall not enter into marriage with them, neither shall they with you, for surely they will turn away your heart after their gods." Solomon clung to these in love. [3] He had 700 wives, who were princesses, and 300 concubines. And his wives turned away his heart. [4] For when Solomon was old his wives turned away his heart after other gods, and his heart was not wholly true to the Lord his God, as was the heart of David his father. [5] For Solomon went after Ashtoreth the goddess of the Sidonians, and after Milcom the abomination of the Ammonites. [6] So Solomon did what was evil in the sight of the Lord and did not wholly follow the Lord, as David his father had done. [7] Then Solomon built a high place for Chemosh the abomination of Moab, and for Molech the abomination of the Ammonites, on the mountain east of Jerusalem. [8] And so he did for all his foreign wives, who made offerings and sacrificed to their gods. [9] And the Lord was angry with Solomon, because his heart had turned away from the Lord, the God of Israel, who had appeared to him twice.

1) **What were God's instructions on marriage (v. 2)? Why?**

God says no to interfaith marriage. The reason is because verse 2 says that it will surely (not maybe) turn your heart away.

2) What caused Solomon's heart to be turned away from God?

His foreign wives.

3) What did Solomon end up doing (v. 6)?

He did what was evil in the sight of the Lord and fell into idolatry.

4) How did God feel about all this?

God felt anger towards Solomon (v. 9).

5) What if an Israelite, during Solomon's time, felt that his faith is strong enough to disobey God's instructions and marry "foreign women" and still not turn away from God? How would you advise such a person?

Verse 2 already says "surely" interfaith marriage will cause your heart to "turn." To even consider disobeying God's Word already proves that this person's faith is not strong.

CASE STUDY 2: King Ahab's interfaith marriage with Jezebel

1 Kings 16:25-33 (ESV)

[25] Omri did what was evil in the sight of the Lord, and did more evil than all who were before him. [26] For he walked in all the way of Jeroboam the son of Nebat, and in the sins that he made Israel to sin, provoking the Lord, the God of Israel, to anger by their idols. [27] Now the rest of the acts of Omri that he did, and the might that he showed, are they not written in the Book of the Chronicles of the Kings of Israel? [28] And Omri slept with his fathers and was buried in Samaria, and Ahab his son reigned in his place. [29] In the thirty-eighth year of Asa king of Judah, Ahab the son of Omri began to reign over Israel, and Ahab the son of Omri reigned over Israel in Samaria twenty-two years. [30] And Ahab the son of Omri did evil in the sight of the Lord, more than all who were before him. [31] And as if it had been a light thing for him to walk in the sins of Jeroboam the son of Nebat, he took for his wife Jezebel the daughter of Ethbaal king of the Sidonians, and went and served Baal and worshiped him. [32] He erected an altar for Baal in the house of Baal, which he built in Samaria. [33] And Ahab made an Asherah. Ahab did more to provoke the Lord, the God of Israel, to anger than all the kings of Israel who were before him.

Background: Jeroboam is the first king that led the newly divided kingdom of Israel into idolatry with two golden calves (one in Bethel and one in Dan) – 1 Kings 12:25-33.

1) Read v. 26. Omri followed Jeroboam's example in sinning. What sin is that?

The sin of idolatry.

2) Read v. 31. Omri's son, Ahab, also followed Jeroboam's example in sinning, but added to that grave sin is another grave sin. What is that?

His interfaith marriage with Jezebel.

3) What did Jezebel introduce to Ahab and Israel?

Baal worship.

4) How did that make God feel?

God felt anger (v. 33).

Part 2: OT Texts on Interfaith Marriages (Ezra-Nehemiah)

Ezra 10:2-3 (ESV)

[2] And Shecaniah the son of Jehiel, of the sons of Elam, addressed Ezra: "We have **broken faith** with our God and have **married foreign women** from the peoples of the land, but even now there is hope for Israel in spite of this. [3] Therefore let us make a covenant with our God to put away all these wives and their children, according to the counsel of my lord and of those who tremble at the commandment of our God, and let it be done according to the Law.

1) How did the people "broke faith?" (v. 2)

Under Ezra's leadership, interfaith marriage is considered an act of unfaithfulness, or adulterous.

Nehemiah 13:23-31 (ESV)

[23] In those days also I saw the Jews who had married women of Ashdod, Ammon, and Moab. [24] And half of their children spoke the language of Ashdod, and they could not speak the language of Judah, but only the language of each people. [25] And I confronted them and cursed them and beat some of them and pulled out their hair. And I made them take an oath in the name of God, saying, "You shall not give your daughters to their sons, or take their daughters for your sons or for yourselves. [26] Did not Solomon king of Israel sin on account of such women? Among the many nations there was no king like him, and he was beloved by his God, and God made him king over all Israel. Nevertheless, foreign women made even him to sin. [27] Shall we then listen to you and do all this great evil and act treacherously against our God by marrying foreign women?" [28] And one of the sons of Jehoiada, the son of Eliashib the high priest, was the son-in-law of Sanballat the Horonite. Therefore I chased him from me. [29] Remember them, O my God, because they have desecrated the priesthood and the covenant of the priesthood and the Levites. [30] Thus I cleansed them from everything foreign, and I established the duties of the priests and Levites, each in his work; [31] and I provided for the wood offering at appointed times, and for the firstfruits.

2) What was it that Nehemiah found to be so detestable? Why?

Under Nehemiah's leadership, interfaith marriage is so detestable that it is worthy of being beaten up and having hair pulled out.

The Israelites knew God's law against interfaith marriage, yet they knowingly went against God's law and intermarried outside of God's covenant community. It is not wrong to marry foreigners as long as they convert first (become proselytes). It is also not wrong if both are not God's people when they get married but along the way, one partner converts. So, what is presented here are interfaith marriages which came about as a result of willful disobedience to God.

The Point:

**The OT consistently portrays interfaith marriage as a huge negative.
It is willful disobedience toward God with severe consequences:
provoking God to anger and falling away to idolatry.**

SESSION THREE

Recap:

- ❖ Previously, we started off by looking at Exodus 34 and Deuteronomy 7, which show us that this prohibition against interfaith marriage is part of Moses's Law and its strong connection with idolatry.

- ❖ Then we looked at how King Solomon, as well as King Ahab, were led astray to idolatry through interfaith marriages, and in so doing, provoked God to anger.

- ❖ Then we looked into Ezra and Nehemiah and again saw a consistent message against interfaith marriages.

NT Texts on Interfaith Marriages

2 Corinthians 6:13-14 (ESV)

[13]In return (I speak as to children) widen your hearts also.

[14]Do not be unequally yoked with unbelievers. For what partnership has righteousness with lawlessness? Or what fellowship has light with darkness?

1) What do you think Paul is talking about in v. 13?

Paul is pleading with the Corinthians to widen their hearts to him because he is trying to convince them that he is a true apostle of Jesus Christ. So, Paul is essentially saying, "Please open wide your hearts to me!" On the one hand, Paul urges them to open their hearts to him, and on the other hand, he is also pleading with the Corinthians not to open their hearts to false teachers who are leading them toward idolatry. So, the famous 2 Corinthians 6:14 is situated in the midst of a false teacher and idolatry context. Paul is instructing the Corinthians not to be unequally yoked with the false teachers.

2) Since the context surrounding this unequally yoked passage is not specifically addressing marriages, is it still appropriate to apply this unequally yoked principle to the marriage context?

The context surrounding the unequally yoked passage is indeed not about marriages, yet it is still very appropriate to apply this unequally yoked principle to the marriage context because essentially, the unequally yoked principle is saying: whoever you open your heart to, you will be like that person. So the principle can still be applied to a marriage context.

3) Is there an interfaith marriage prohibition verse in the New Testament that is specifically written in the marriage context?

It is true that because 2 Corinthians 6:14 is not a passage that is specifically targeting a marriage context, the argument is weaker, and you will have a hard time using such a verse to convince somebody who is already contemplating entering into an unequally yoked relationship. So, the better plan is to direct such a person to a New Testament text that specifically addresses the marriage context. And for such a New Testament text, we go to 1 Corinthians 7:39.

1 Corinthians 7:39 (NIV)

[39] A woman is bound to her husband as long as he lives. But if her husband dies, she is free to marry anyone she wishes, but he must belong to the Lord.

4) How would you interpret such a verse?

Remember that this is a New Testament text that is specifically addressing the context of marriage. Here, Paul is giving instructions to Christian widows, telling them that if they were to remarry, they have to make sure that the new spouse "belongs to the Lord," meaning the new spouse must be a Christian.

This is a clear and direct verse that gives us the confidence to believe that the Old Testament prohibition on interfaith marriages still stands today, in the New Testament era.

Ephesians 5:22-32 (ESV)

[22] Wives, submit to your own husbands, as to the Lord. [23] For the husband is the head of the wife even as Christ is the head of the church, his body, and is himself its Savior. [24] Now as the church submits to Christ, so also wives should submit in everything to their husbands. [25] Husbands, love your wives, as Christ loved the church and gave himself up for her, [26] that he might sanctify her, having cleansed her by the washing of water with the word, [27] so that he might present the church to himself in splendor, without spot or wrinkle or any such thing, that she might be holy and without blemish. [28] In the same way husbands should love their wives as their own bodies. He who loves his wife loves himself. [29] For no one ever hated his own flesh, but nourishes and cherishes it, just as Christ does the church, [30] because we are members of his body. [31] "Therefore a man shall leave his father and mother and hold fast to his wife, and the two shall become one flesh." [32] This mystery is profound, and I am saying that it refers to Christ and the church.

5) For the Christian, what is marriage meant to reflect?

Christ and the Church.

6) Can an interfaith marriage reflect this God-given picture of marriage?

All Christian marriages ought to aspire toward such a glorious picture of marriage (Christ and the Church), but an interfaith couple simply cannot, in unison, aspire toward such a glorious picture of marriage.

The Point:

**For those who demand NT evidence
that the interfaith marriage prohibition still stands,
you can offer them these passages, particularly 1 Corinthians 7:39.
At the same time, be mindful that there is not a single verse in the NT
that even remotely suggests that the prohibition has been lifted.
So, it is clear that the prohibition is there in the OT and also in the NT.
Therefore, to enter into an unequally yoked relationship
is to disobey Scripture and that is a sin.**

Group Discussion

1) Share one practical way to avoid getting into an unequally yoked relationship.

Do not spend extended one-to-one time with a non-Christian unnecessarily (this would include avoiding going out on dates with non-Christians). Keep away from such arrangements, as feelings could develop from such settings.

2) List all the practical problems you can think of which may arise when a Christian gets into an unequally yoked marriage relationship.

Some examples: differences in the understanding of male headship, differences in the understanding of biblical "leave and cleave" resulting in in-law issues, career options (wrong priorities), expenditure of funds and resources (conflict with regards to giving to gospel work), entertainment and leisure (different values), how to raise children (different values), different opinions on how to spend the weekends or holidays (signing up for church camps and attending weekly Sunday School may be considered a waste of time for the unbelieving partner), not able to pray together during tough times, conflict of ideas in arranging for the wedding or funerals.

All marriages are tough. For the Christian marriage, at least there is a common ground–a common basis (Scripture) whereby differences can be resolved through applying biblical principles.

3) **How should we advise Christians who feel tempted to get into an unequally yoked relationship?**

Study God's Word for themselves, especially: 1 Corinthians 7:39 and 2 Corinthians 6:13-14. Find a godly accountability partner.

4) **How should we treat Christians who are already attached or married to an unbeliever?**

Accept them as they are and treat them with love, kindness, understanding, and compassion. We are, in fact, fellow sinners, since we too may be sinning in other areas.

Temptation to get a non-Christian boyfriend/girlfriend is very different from other forms of temptation. For example, stealing. Imagine you stole money. You know stealing is wrong. You know it is a sin, and after a while, the guilt sets in, and you feel bad about it and then you repent of stealing and ask God for forgiveness and return the stolen money. However, the temptation toward an interfaith attachment is different because you cannot hide it. You can hide stolen money but you cannot hide your relationship. Sooner or later, your Christian friends are going to bump into you holding hands with your non-Christian girlfriend or boyfriend. So instead of hiding it, people tend to want to justify their unequally yoked relationships, and that is what makes this such a big problem. Most of the time, they will say, "Nowhere in the NT says that it is a sin. Interfaith marriage is only a sin in the OT; in the NT, nothing is said of it, so it is not wrong." They tend to justify it and then continue going to church. Churches that are more liberal do not talk about such things; nobody in such churches knows what is the stand on such things. So, the couple will likely continue going to church like nothing is wrong. However, there are churches that are stricter and clearer about such teachings and have policies where those involved in unequally yoked relationships cannot serve in the church. The church will require them to step down from ministry. For churches like that, the couple would tend to leave the church and go find a laxer church or stop going to church altogether. And when they do that, they lose their spiritual support, which would be worse for them. Already, they are not spiritually strong, and yet they are moving away from their spiritual family. Therefore, it is best to advise people who got involved in an unequally yoked romantic relationship to not stop attending church and to continue surrounding themselves with Christian friends. For them, the temptation to drop out of all things Christian will be very strong, so we need to encourage them to persevere in the faith and stick with their community of faith.

This unequally yoked issue does have a tendency
to drive Christians away from the church,
so our number one thought should be how to help the unequally yoked
stay in the church–how to help them feel accepted,
even in the midst of their sin.
This is tough because people tend to feel judged
when they are in such a sin and attending church at the same time.

OPEN BOOK TEST

Q1) Your schoolmate refuses to believe that the Law of Moses prohibits interfaith marriage. List two places in Scripture that you can point out to this schoolmate of yours.

Exodus 34:11-17 and Deuteronomy 7:3-4

Q2) Which chapter in 1 Kings records God's anger with King Solomon's interfaith marriages?

Chapter 11

Q3) Which chapter in 1 Kings records God's anger with King Ahab for his interfaith marriage with Jezebel?

Chapter 16

Q4) Where in the book of Ezra do we see interfaith marriage being understood as unfaithfulness?

Ezra 10:2

Q5) Which chapter in the book of Nehemiah do we see Nehemiah being so mad at the people's interfaith marriages?

Chapter 13

Q6) Your non-Christian friend just came across the term "unequally yoked" and ask you if that term is even found in the Bible. Where can you direct her to find it in the Bible?

2 Corinthians 6:14

Q7) That same non-Christian friend kept insisting that using the "unequally yoked' principle on marriage is to use it out of context. What other verse in the New Testament can you direct her to?

1 Corinthians 7:39

Bibliography

Ash, Christopher. *Married for God: Making Your Marriage the Best It Can Be.* Nottingham: IVP, 2007.

Ashley, Timothy R. *The Book of Numbers.* New International Commentary on the Old Testament, ed. Robert L. Hubbard. Grand Rapids: Eerdmans Publishing, 1993. Olive Tree Edition.

Barnett, Paul. *The Second Epistle to the Corinthians.* New International Commentary on the New Testament, eds. Ned B. Stonehouse, F. F. Bruce, and Gordon D. Fee. Grand Rapids: Eerdmans Publishing, 1997. Olive Tree Edition.

Baumert, Lisa. "Biblical Interpretation and the Epistle to the Ephesians." *Priscilla Papers* 31, no. 4 (Fall 2017): 28–32.

Beard, Colin, and John P. Wilson. *Experiential Learning: A Handbook for Education, Training and Coaching.* 3rd ed. London: Kogan Page, 2013.

Berchie, Daniel. "Marrying an 'Unbelieving' Partner: An Exegetical Study of 2 Corinthians 6:14." *Valley View University Journal of Theology* 3 (2014): 61–77.

Ciampa, Roy E., and Brian S. Rosner. *The First Letter to the Corinthians.* The Pillar New Testament Commentary, ed. D.A. Carson. Grand Rapids: Eerdmans Publishing, 2010. Olive Tree Edition.

Clinton, Tim, and Chap Clark. *The Quick-Reference Guide to Counseling Teenagers.* Grand Rapids: Baker Books, 2010.

Cloud, Henry, and John Townsend. *Boundaries in Dating: How Healthy Choices Grow Healthy Relationships.* Grand Rapids: Zondervan, 2000.

Craigie, Peter C. *The Book of Deuteronomy.* New International Commentary on the Old Testament, ed. Robert L. Hubbard. Grand Rapids: Eerdmans, 1976. Olive Tree Edition.

Davids, Peter H. *The First Epistle of Peter.* New International Commentary on the Old Testament, ed. Robert L. Hubbard. Grand Rapids: Eerdmans Publishing, 1990. Olive Tree Edition.

Fee, Gordon D. *The First Epistle to the Corinthians.* New International Commentary on the New Testament, eds. Ned B. Stonehouse, F. F. Bruce, and Gordon D. Fee. Grand Rapids: Eerdmans Publishing, 2014. Olive Tree Edition.

Fensham, F. Charles. *The Books of Ezra and Nehemiah.* New International Commentary on the Old Testament, ed. Robert L. Hubbard. Grand Rapids: Eerdmans Publishing, 1983. Olive Tree Edition.

Fitzmyer, Joseph A. *First Corinthians.* The Anchor Yale Bible Commentaries, ed. John J. Collins. New Haven: Yale University Press, 2008.

Fong, Michelle. "Using Technology to Support Discussions on Sensitive Topics in the Study of Business Ethics." *Journal of Information Technology Education, Research* 14 (January 1, 2015): 243–56.

Garland, David E. *1 Corinthians.* Baker Exegetical Commentary on the New Testament, eds. Robert W. Yarbrough and Joshua W. Jipp. Grand Rapids: Baker Academic, 2003.

Goldingay, John. *Genesis.* Baker Commentary on the Old Testament: Pentateuch, ed. Bill Arnold. Grand Rapids: Baker Academic, 2020.

Hamilton, Victor P. *The Book of Genesis.* New International Commentary on the Old Testament, ed. Robert L. Hubbard. Grand Rapids: Eerdmans Publishing, 1990. Olive Tree Edition.

Harris, Murray J. *The Second Epistle to the Corinthians.* The New International Greek Testament Commentary, ed. Mark Goodacre and Todd D. Still. Grand Rapids: Eerdmans Publishing, 2013. Olive Tree Edition.

Jůvová, Alena, and Ondřej Duda. "Emotional Intelligence Factors Helping Teachers Cope with Emotionally Tense Situations and Enhancing Effective Pedagogical Communication." *E-Pedagogium* 21, no. 2 (April 2021): 18–32.

Keller, Timothy. *The Meaning of Marriage: Facing the Complexities of Commitment with the Wisdom of God. London:* Hodder and Stoughton, 2011.

Kruse, Colin G. *Paul's Letter to the Romans.* The Pillar New Testament Commentary, ed. D. A. Carson. Grand Rapids: Eerdmans Publishing, 2012. Olive Tree Edition.

Mathews, Kenneth A. *Genesis 11:27-50:26.* The New American Commentary, ed. E. Ray Clendenen, vol. 1B. Nashville: Broadman & Holman Publishers, 2005.

McDougall, Donald G. "Unequally Yoked–a Re-Examination of 2 Corinthians 6:11-7:4." *The Master's Seminary Journal* 10, no. 1 (Spr 1999): 113–37.

Merrill, Eugene H. *Deuteronomy.* The New American Commentary, ed. E. Ray Clendenen. Nashville: Holman Reference, 1994.

Miller, Patrick D. "Divine Command/Divine Law: A Biblical Perspective." *Studies in Christian Ethics* 23, no. 1 (February 2010): 21–34.

Parker, Clinton, III. "Pastoral Role Modeling as an Antecedent to Corporate Spirituality." *Journal of Religious Leadership* 13, no. 1 (Spr 2014): 161–85.

Regnerus, Mark, Naomi Schaefer Riley, and Russell D. Moore. "Biblical Bonding: Is Interfaith Marriage Always Wrong, Given That the Bible Teaches Us Not to Be 'Unequally Yoked'?" *Christianity Today* 57, no. 5 (June 2013): 62–63.

Russell, Beth S., Champika K. Soysa, Marc J. Wagoner, and Lori Dawson. "Teaching Prevention on Sensitive Topics: Key Elements and Pedagogical Techniques." *Journal of Primary Prevention* 29, no. 5 (September 1, 2008): 413–33.

Schreiner, Thomas R. *1 Corinthians*. Tyndale New Testament Commentaries, ed. David G. Firth. Downers Grove: IVP Academic, 2018.

Scolnic, Benjamin Edidin. "Master of Life: Why God Commands Abraham to Sacrifice Isaac (Gen. 22)." *Jewish Bible Quarterly* 48, no. 3 (July 2020): 185–95.

Silberman, Israela. "Spiritual Role Modeling: The Teaching of Meaning Systems." *The International Journal for the Psychology of Religion* 13, no. 3 (2003): 175–95.

Snyman, Fanie. "Investigating the Issue of Mixed Marriages in Malachi, Ezra-Nehemiah and the Pentateuch." *Scriptura* 116, no. 2 (2017): 175–87.

Starcher, Keith. "Intentionally Building Rapport With Students." *College Teaching* 59, no. 4 (Fall 2011): 162.

Starling, David Ian. "The Ἄπιστοι of 2 Cor 6:14: Beyond the Impasse." *Novum Testamentum* 55, no. 1 (2013): 45–60.

Strobel, Lee, and Leslie Strobel. *Spiritual Mismatch: Hope for Christians Married to Someone Who Doesn't Know God*. Grand Rapids: Zondervan, 2017.

Stuart, Douglas K. *Exodus*, vol. 2. The New American Commentary, ed. E. Ray Clendenen. Nashville: Holman Reference, 2006. Olive Tree Edition.

Thiselton, Anthony C. *The First Epistle to the Corinthians*. The New International Greek Testament Commentary, ed. Mark Goodacre and Todd D. Still. Grand Rapids: Eerdmans Publishing, 2013. Olive Tree Edition.

Waltke, Bruce K. *The Book of Proverbs: Chapters 1-15*. New International Commentary on the Old Testament, ed. Robert L. Hubbard. Grand Rapids: Eerdmans Publishing, 2004. Olive Tree Edition.

Webb, William J. "Unequally Yoked Together with Unbelievers." *Bibliotheca Sacra* 149, no. 594 (April 1992): 162–179.

Wiseman, Donald J. *1 and 2 Kings*. Tyndale Old Testament Commentaries, ed. David G. Firth. Downers Grove: IVP Academic, 2008. Olive Tree Edition.

Wong, David W. F. *The Unequal Yoke: When Two May Not Walk Together*. Singapore: Genesis Books, 2013.

Yancey, George A. "Unequally Yoked by Race or by Faith?" *Criswell Theological Review* 6, no. 2 (Spr 2009): 65–75.

Scripture Index

WHY

Cannot?

Scriptural View
of
Christians
Dating and Marrying
Non-Christians